Pictorial Encyclopedia of
Historic Architectural
Plans, Details and Elements

JOHN THEODORE HANEMAN

Pictorial Encyclopedia of Historic Architectural Plans, Details and Elements

WITH 1,880 LINE DRAWINGS OF ARCHES, DOMES, DOORWAYS, FACADES, GABLES, WINDOWS, ETC.

Dover Publications, Inc., New York

Published in Canada by General Publishing Company, Ltd., 30 Lesmill Road, Don Mills, Toronto, Ontario.

Published in the United Kingdom by Constable and Company, Ltd., 10 Orange Street, London WC2H 7EG.

This Dover edition, first published in 1984, is an unabridged and unaltered republication of *A Manual of Architectural Compositions: 70 Plates with 1,880 Examples,* first published by The Architectural Book Publishing Co., Paul Wenzel & Maurice Krakow, N.Y., in 1923.

Manufactured in the United States of America
Dover Publications, Inc., 31 East 2nd Street, Mineola, N.Y. 11501

Library of Congress Cataloging in Publication Data

Haneman, John Theodore.
  Pictorial encyclopedia of historic architectural plans, details and elements.

  "With 1,880 line drawings of arches, domes, doorways, façades, gables, windows, etc."
  Reprint. Originally published: A manual of architectural compositions. New York : Architectural Book Pub. Co., 1923.
  Bibliography: p.
  Includes index.
  1. Architecture—Details. 2. Architecture—Composition, proportion, etc. I. Title.
NA284O.H34   1984   721   83-20622
ISBN 0-486-24605-1

8.7.85 AC

TO
F . C . P . H .

*   *   *

Haec olim meminisse juvabit.

FOREWORD

This book is a collection of architectural compositions, arranged and grouped in convenient reference form with the express purpose of furnishing suggestion and inspiration to those interested with the solution of architectural problems.

Only the fundamentals, and their simplest variants are shown; as the final development is directly dependent on individual interpretation and invention.

CONTENTS

With the subjects tabulated according to their particular purposes

CONTENTS (Continued)

In compiling this work the following books have been consulted:

Anderson — Italian Renaissance Architecture. English Country Houses. Belcher & Macartney—Later Renaissance. Concours Rougevin et Godeboeuf. Corroyer—L'Architecture Gothique. Cram—American Country Houses of To-Day. Duncan—Country Houses. Durand—Recueil et Parallel. Flagg—Small Houses. Gayet—L'Art Arabe. Gromort—Éléments d' Architecture Classique. Guadet— Éléments et Théorie de l'Architecture. Hoepli—Il Legno, Il Ferro, Lo Stucco, Nell' Arte Italiana. Kidder—Building Construction & Superintendence. Les Grands Prix de Rome d'Architecture. Letarouilly—Édifices de Rome Moderne. Leyland— Gardens Old & New. Lowell—Smaller Italian Villas & Farm Houses. Meyer— Handbook of Ornament. Nash—The Mansions of England in the Olden Time. de Neufforge—Recueil Élémentaire d'Architecture. Prang—Illustrations of the History of Art. Prentice—Renaissance Architecture & Ornament in Spain. Reber—A History of Ancient Art. Rieth—Skizzen. Sauvageot—Palais, Châteaux, Hotels, et Maisons de France. Schaefer—Die Holzarchiketur Deutschlands. Schünemann—Bremen und seine Bauten. Sturgis—A Dictionary of Architecture and Building. Thomas & Fallon—North Italian Details. Uhde—Baudenkmaeler in Spanien und Portugal. Vallance—Art in England during the Elizabethan and Stuart Periods. Weaver—Small Country Houses of To-Day. Wilson—Cathedrals of France.

Pictorial Encyclopedia of
Historic Architectural
Plans, Details and Elements

ARCADES

The common use of the term arcade, is for a considerable number of arches used structurally or decoratively in some architectural composition.

1   An arcade of piers. Plan showing the pier and column in combination.

2   Alternating piers and columns.

3   Arcade of columns, also grouped alternating with piers.

4   Arcade with an engaged order.

5   Arcade with a coupled engaged order.

6–7   Arcades interrupted with piers.

8   Piers and columns staggered in plan.

9   An arcade with interlacing arches.

10   An interior arcade of columns between piers with vertical emphasis.

11   An arcade wherein a smaller one is combined.

12   Large and small columns combined in an interlacing arcade.

13   An arcade on an incline.

14   An arcade with a smaller similar motive superimposed in the pier space.

15   Superimposed arches in an arcade.

16   An arcade within a large arch motive.

17   Superimposed arcades with pointed arches. Columns above piers.

18   Superimposed arcades, columns above column-piers.

19–20   Superimposed engaged orders with arcades between.

21   A colonnade between orders with a smaller similar motive above but with twice the number of arches.

22   Superimposed coupled arches in an arcade motive.

23   A small arcade motive with a larger one above.

24   Small arcades, pointed arches upon columns, above one another.

25   Superimposed arcades of five stories.

26   Superimposed arcades with orders in a facade composition.

Plate 1

ARCHES

The arch is a mechanical means of spanning an opening by wedged shaped solids, keeping one another in position, and transforming the vertical pressure of the superimposed load into components transmitted laterally to the abutments.

1–2–3   Archaic examples of openings with corbeled heads, but not true arches.

4   A curved lintel springing from corbels. "Bell arch."

5   Carved head corbels, not a true arch.

6   Primitive form of true arch.

7   Earliest use of the keystone.

8   A "Flat arch" with a segmental "Relieving arch."

9   Pointed arches. "Equilateral," "Lancet," "Drop."

9a   With dissimilar intrados and extrados. "Tuscan arch."

10   A "Round headed arch" with voussoirs.

11   A "Three centered arch," or "Basket-handle arch."

12   A "Flat arch."

13   A "Stilted arch," in which the center is higher than the impost of the arch.

14   A "Horse-shoe arch," in which the opening is greater than a semi circle.

15   A pointed "Four centered arch." "Tudor arch."

16   "Skew sided arches."

17–18   Pointed "Foiled," or "Cusped arches."

19   A pointed horse-shoe arch. "Indian," or "Persian arch."

20   An "Ogee arch" with curves of counter flexture.

21–22–23   Variations of arch outlines.

24   Semi circular extrados with an irregularly ornamented intrados.

25   Interlaced horse-shoe arches.

26   Interlaced arches composed of cusps, points and rounds.

27   Interlacing cusped and horse-shoe arches in combination.

28   Superimposed arches, a horse-shoe arch above a multi-foil cusped arch.

29   Concentric round headed arches.

30   Superimposed pointed arches with elaborated cuspings.

Plate 2

ARCHES

The Commemorative or Triumphal arch, as its title indicates, was a composition of one or more arches, serving as a monument, commemorative of some particular occurrence, or as a gate, through which the ancient triumphal processions proceeded.

1   A single opening with a composition of horizontal bands.

2   A mass with a single opening in which the order, an attic and statuary are introduced at the corners for embellishment.

3   Coupled orders and statuary flanking an opening.

4   Two pyramidal masses flanking an opening.

5   An order and attic composition framing a single opening, but with greater emphasis at the opening, obtained by projection.

6   Coupled orders and attic flanking an opening.

7   Orders flanking an opening with a superimposed lesser order in an attic.

8–11–12   Superimposed orders in composition with a single opening.

9   Orders and horizontal bands about a single opening with a double attic for central emphasis.

10   A pylon with a small similar one about a single opening.

13   Two openings in a large mass separated by a column.

14   Two openings in a mass crowned with a cornice, arcaded and colonnaded attics respectively.

15   Coupled orders flanking two openings, the mass emphasized at the corners in the upper part by single orders, the whole crowned with a cornice and attic.

16   Two openings with pedimented orders in a composition with an enriched attic.

17   Three openings in a simple mass, with the central opening made greater and more important by projecting beyond the main mass.

18   A large opening flanked by small ones in a simple mass in a composition of panels, high relief and an entablature.

19   Pyramidal flanking masses with small central openings and a small central motive with the greater opening.

20   A mass with a large central opening and a smaller one at each side, bands at the spring of the central arch, architrave and corner emphasis with an entablature and an attic.

21   Orders framing triple openings. The central arch being higher and further emphasized with a pediment. Carving in high relief upon the surface. The whole terminated with attic and triple pedestals supporting statuary.

22   A large central and smaller side arches within an order composition, with an attic and group of statuary at the center.

23   Three equal openings in an order and attic composition, the center emphasized with a statuary group at the top.

24   Three openings within coupled orders, flanking pedimented niches for statuary; a simple attic terminating the whole.

25   Four openings in an oblong mass, crowned with a colonnaded arcade supporting an attic.

Plate 3

BALCONIES

The balcony is a platform projecting from the wall of a building, enclosed by a parapet or balustrade and supported upon brackets, corbels, projecting members of wood, metal, or masonry.

1   A rostrum within an arch and at the head of a flight of steps.

2   A rostrum in front of an opening and at the head of a flight of steps on each side.

3–4   A covered rostrum at the head of a flight of steps.

5   The landing at the head of a semi-circular flight of steps serving as a rostrum.

6   A pulpit attached to the side of a column with steps spiraling around the shaft.

7   A balcony supported upon columns.

8   Superimposed balconies supported upon arches.

9   A balcony placed in a wall niche.

10   A free standing pulpit supported by columns.

11   A balcony incorporated in the facade of a building.

12   A metal balcony with a metal support.

13   A metal balcony within a window reveal.

14   A balcony with masonry parapet supported upon a masonry base.

15   A masonry balcony supported upon arches corbeled beyond the wall face.

16   A balustered balcony supported upon brackets projecting beyond the surface of the wall.

17   Two-storied metal balconies resting upon metal brackets.

18   An enclosed or screened balcony upon a bracket.

19   A balcony at the corner of a building supported by a column.

20   A corner balcony supported upon corbeled arches.

21   A corner balcony supported upon brackets.

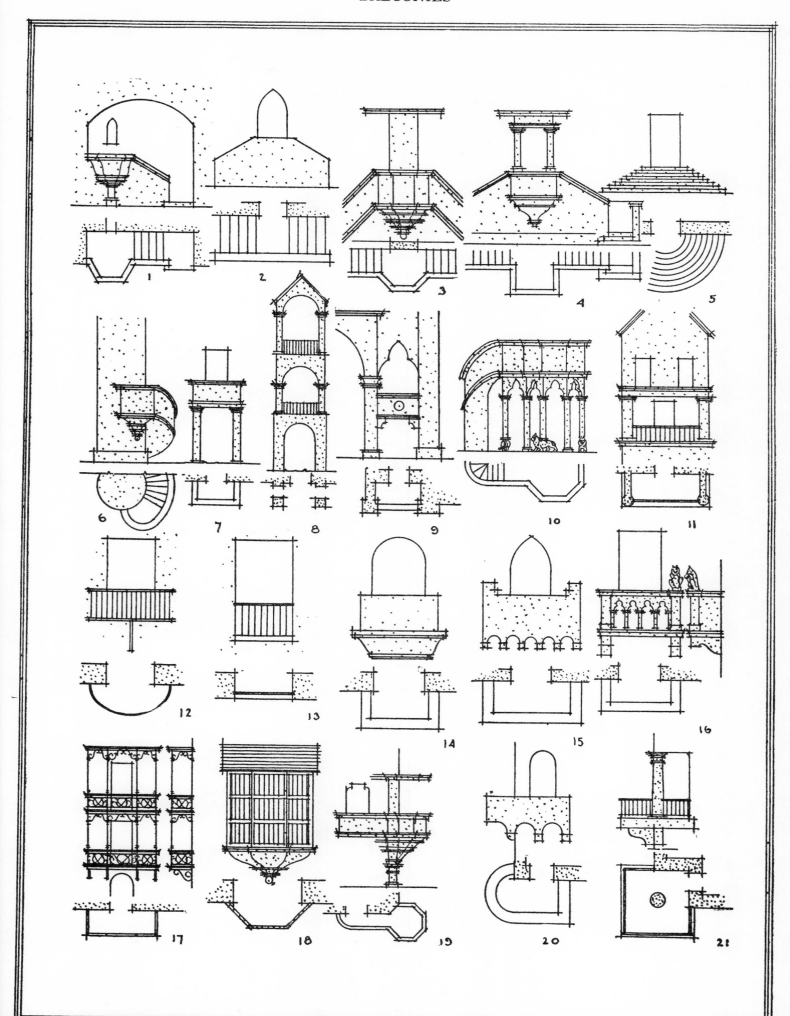

Plate **4**

BAYS

The bay is an architectural motive of one or more stories repeated laterally in a facade. Also a recess or opening in walls.

Dealing with one and two storied motives.

1–5–6 Motive with base and cornice divided by vertical rustication.

2 Columns and entablature forming a bay.

3 An order with a balustrade forming a motive.

4 A high base with pilasters, entablature and attic.

7 An opening flanked with coupled orders and the use of balusters and statuary in the opening.

8 An order extending through two stories interrupting horizontal courses.

9 Semi circular towers springing from a sloping base.

10–11 Vertical divisions made by buttresses, with the horizontal bands carried around them.

12 A colonnade upon a high base with statuary introduced for emphasis.

13 Engaged columns with individual pedestals flanking openings.

14 Similar grouped openings above one another with horizontal bands.

15 Arches upon piers upon a high base.

16 A superimposed colonnade with opening groups between.

Arches between the columns of superimposed colonnades.

18 Coupled openings between superimposed coupled colonnades.

19 Superimposed arcades.

20–21 Coupled arches with openings above.

22 Superimposed colonnades with an arcade in the lower and a circular headed opening in the upper.

23 A high base with openings and a colonnade above with large openings between the columns and above those in the base.

24 An arcaded basement with a superimposed arcade within a colonnade.

25 An arcaded base with a superimposed arcade within a colonnade, with a sub-order and balustrade as an enrichment.

26 Arches between the columns of a colonnade, with statuary used as a column emphasis. Openings above the arches and a balustrade and entablature terminating the whole.

27 A gable between buttresses, with a circular opening above coupled circular headed openings.

1

2

3

4

5

6

7

8

9

10

11

12

13

14

15

16

17

18

19

20

21

22

23

24

25

26

27

Plate 5

BAYS

Dealing with three storied motives

1 A rusticated base with a high opening with architrave and pediment above, terminating with a square opening in a frieze.

2 Base, string courses and entablature, separating a small lower opening and two super-imposed arched openings.

3 Coupled orders flanking various sized openings.

4 Similar openings between superimposed orders, with a dormer termination.

5 Similar openings between buttresses, with a dormer termination.

6 Dormers emphasizing large openings above an arcade.

7–8 Plain surfaces emphasized by the grouping of voids above one another.

9 Rustication used as an order with a base and cornice.

10 Superimposed colonnades, the lower extending two stories.

11 Colonnade and arch motive with an attic.

12 Superimposed colonnades of unequal heights, with a band dividing the upper one horizontally.

13 Rustication covering the entire height with a base and cornice.

14–20 A rusticated basement with rustication used as piers for the upper stories, terminated with a cornice and balustrade.

15 Rustication used in the two lower stories, rusticated piers in the upper.

16 Superimposed rusticated piers with horizontal courses.

17 Horizontal division of the facade with rusticated lower story and rusticated piers in the upper, cornice and balustrade termination.

18 Rusticated piers and orders in alternation for two stories, with the piers carried up in the attic.

19 Two lower stories rusticated with the upper emphasized with alternating window motives and vertical rustication.

21 A high base with coupled orders extending two stories, the second story emphasized by the window motives.

22 A base supporting a colonnade extending two stories.

23 Rusticated piers at intervals in the two lower stories, with the piers extending and interrupting a colonnaded arcade in the upper story, crowned with cornice and balustrade.

24 An arcade with superimposed arch motives separated by bands.

25 An arcade with an arched opening above, with rectangular openings in an attic divided by rustication extending the whole height at the corners. Horizontal bands and entablature.

26 Colonnaded basement with horizontal bands dividing the stories.

27 The second story emphasized by an arcade with an order.

28 The basement emphasized with an arcade with order, horizontal bands dividing the stories.

29 Superimposed colonnades, arcades within the two upper ones.

30 A motive with the fenestration dominant.

31 Superimposed arcades, the upper extending two stories.

32 A buttress or pier motive with an arcade in the upper story.

33 Superimposed colonnades of diminishing heights, framing an arcade, pedimented and architraved window and a square one respectively.

34 Superimposed colonnades of coupled columns with arched openings between.

35 A superimposed four column motive of varying heights.

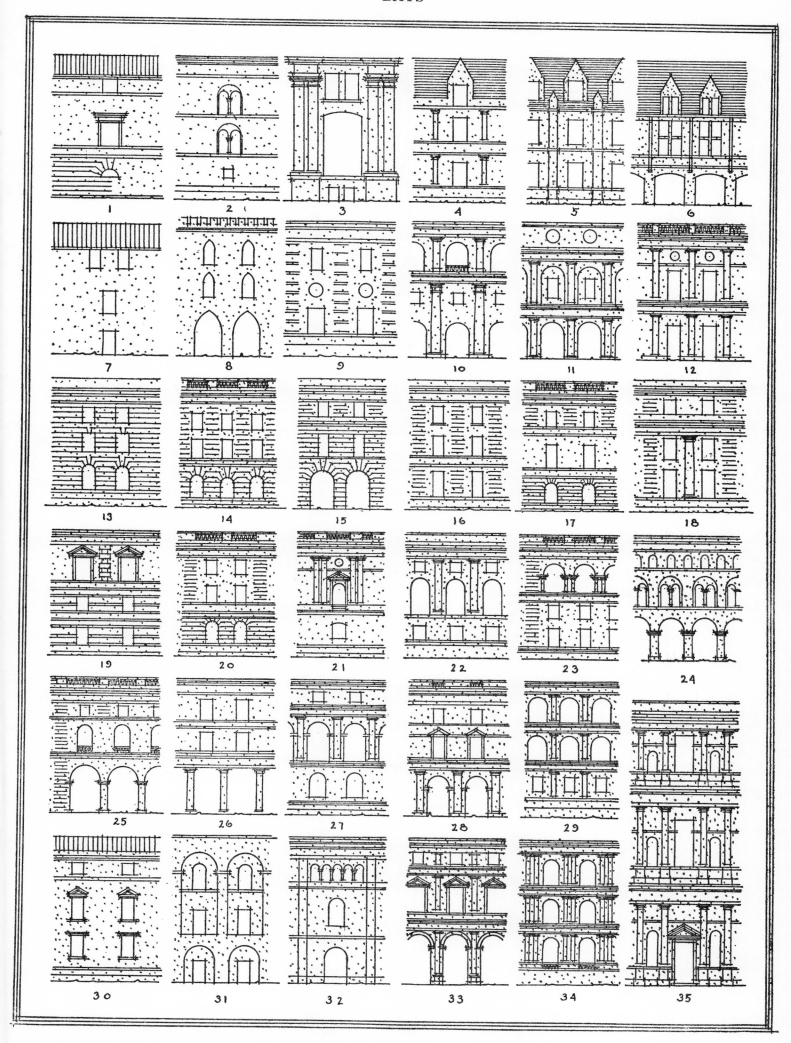

Plate 6

BAYS

Dealing with four stories and more

1 Horizontal bands dividing the facade, with the introduction of columns at the corners of the upper division.

2 Horizontal bands dividing a facade supported upon corbeled arches above a base with a batter wall.

3 Horizontal bands dividing the facade with a colonnade emphasizing the upper division.

4 Heavy horizontal divisions of the facade with colonnades of unequal height in the two upper divisions. Quoins emphasizing the lower story.

5 Colonnades embellishing the two upper stories of a facade, with the lower divided by a string-course and battered wall.

6 A plain basement and mezzanine with a second floor order composition, extending into an attic story.

7–8 Horizontal bands of varying importance in composition with quoins.

9 Horizontal bands dividing the facade in two parts, the upper embellished with a colonnade, balustrade and statuary and more important window treatment.

10 Three horizontal divisions of a facade, the upper two enriched with superimposed columns and a dormer window spaced above the lower voids.

11 Four stories of superimposed colonnades with arches within the lower three.

12 Three stories of superimposed colonnaded arcades, with a coupled column motive for the top story.

13 String courses dividing the facade with relation to the importance of the floors.

14 An arch with a string-course and a frieze motive.

15 Dissimilar voids and groups in composition with superimposed orders.

16 Superimposed order and arcade motive, terminated with a series of gables.

17 Vertical motives between arches terminating in three-storied turrets, which flank coupled arches.

18 A gable between buttresses, pierced by a three-storied coupled-arch motive and a circular void above.

19 Superimposed orders terminating in a gable motive.

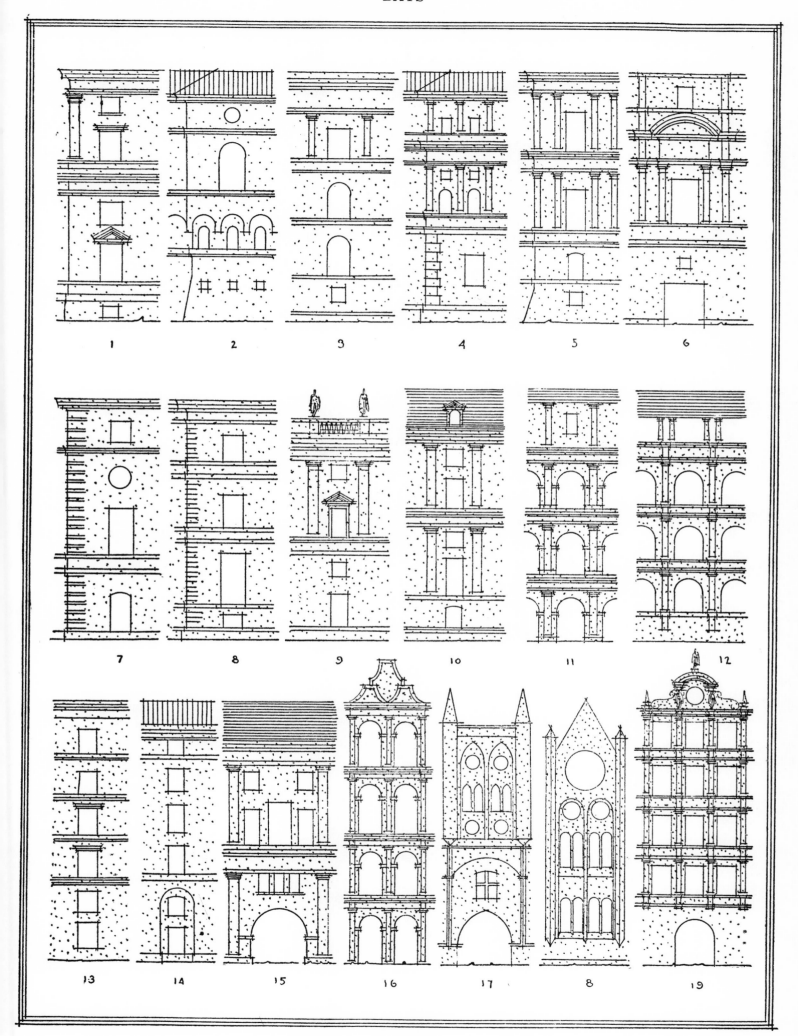

Plate 7

BAYS

Dealing with interior motives

1-9-15 An order upon a base in combination with an attic order.

2 A colonnade within an opening, the entablature continuing along the wall for horizontal emphasis.

3 An arcade with a panelled attic.

4 Panelled pilasters flanking oblong and semi circular panels.

5-6 Vaulted bays divided by arches at the first story.

7-8 Panel compositions crowned with an entablature.

10 An order with panel groups between.

11 Coupled orders flanking panels.

12 A colonnade with entablature with superimposed compositions between, framing statuary.

13 A colonnade within an arch, the colonnade being of secondary importance.

14 A dome on pendentives with arcaded sides.

16 A vaulted bay with vertical emphasis, flanking an arch and open above.

17 A wall arcade with vertical decoration at the piers and an opening above the arch.

18 An arcade within vertical uprights forming the bay with a window group above.

19 A vaulted bay divided by arches on the first and second stories, with a central opening above.

20 A vaulted bay divided in two by a secondary vertical division with openings between.

21 A vaulted bay with vertical emphasis at the sides enclosing superimposed varied openings.

22 An arcade with an order supporting an arcade with vertical expression at regular intervals.

23 A three storied arch composition between vertical two storied emphasis, with the top story the most important.

24 Superimposed colonnades with an attic motive for openings.

25 Superimposed arcades within an arch.

26 An arcade with arched openings in an attic with vault ribs between.

27 Wall piers with niches and panels above, surmounted by an attic with an order or consoles, all flanking openings.

28 A vaulted bay with vertical sides enclosing an arch, arcade and coupled arches respectively.

29-30 Vaulted bays with superimposed arches and arcades with vertical divisions of secondary importance.

1 2 3 4 5 6
7 8 9 10 11 12
13 14 15 16 17 18
19 20 21 22 23 24
25 26 27 28 29 30

Plate 8

BRIDGES

A bridge is a structure spanning more or less of a depression, and used as a means of communication from ridge to ridge.

1   A bridge with lintels spanning piers.

2   A single span, masonry or metal foot bridge.

3   A single span masonry bridge with steps.

4   A covered single span bridge from one building to another.

5   A covered single span bridge, a flight of steps within an arcade.

6   A double span bridge with a central pier support and side embankments.

7   A triple span bridge with pier supports.

8   A triple span covered bridge, with arcades on either side of a driveway.

9   A triple span bridge communicating between two levels with a monumental treatment of colonnades, pediments and stairs.

10   A many spanned pier bridge roofed and arcaded.

11   A many spanned pier bridge with covered arcades at either side of the roadway, and with particular emphasis at the ends.

12   A triple span bridge with embellished piers.

13–14–15   Many spanned bridges with various arch and pier treatments.

16–17–18   Span bridges with various fortified tower compositions.

19   A pier bridge with ornamental emphasis at the piers.

20   A pier bridge of many spans with interlacing arches, large and small roadways enclosed within an arcade.

21   A pier bridge of many spans with dwellings flanking the roadway.

22   Spans upon piers where great height is necessary.

23   A single roadway above superimposed arches.

24   Superimposed arcades with three roadways.

25   Arched spans with an arcade above supporting the roadway.

26   A wall used as a bridge with variously shaped openings to lighten the masonry.

27   Superimposed arches with lateral buttressing at the piers, supporting a roadway divided by an arcade supporting another roadway at a higher level.

28   Superimposed arcades supporting roadways.

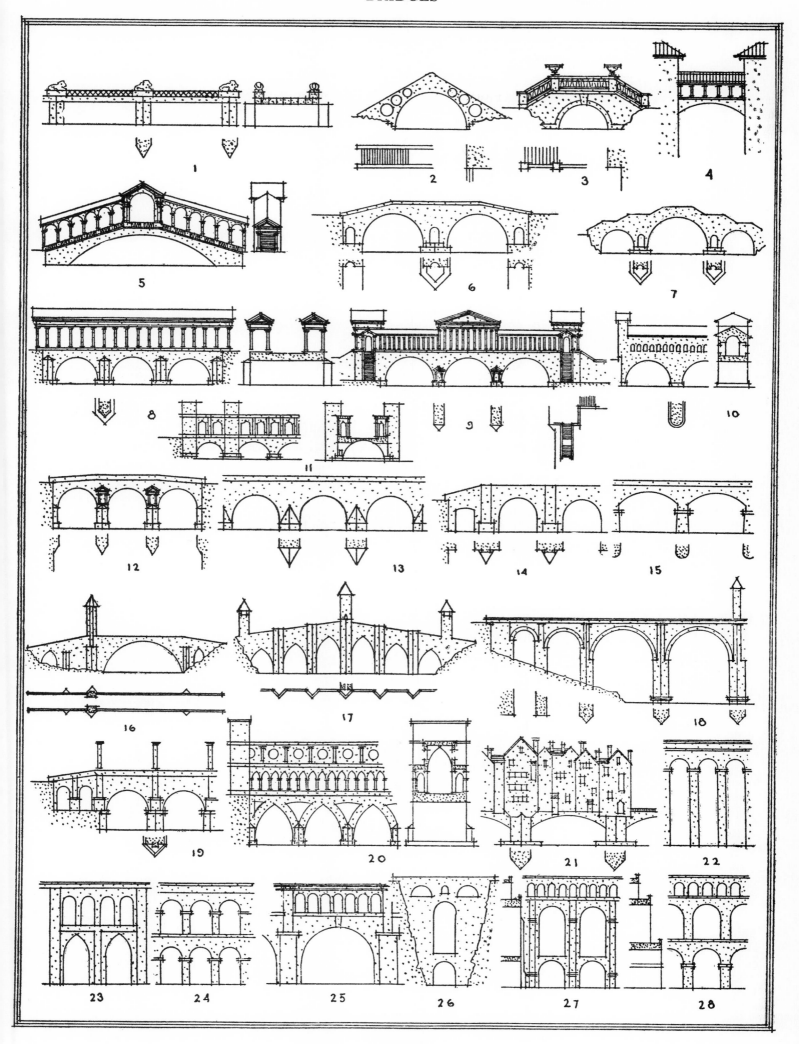

Plate 9

BRIDGES

Dealing with wood and metal types, also with metal and masonry compositions

1   A wooden truss bridge for a small span.

2–3   Wooden truss bridges for medium sized spans.

4   A metal truss bridge.

5   A three span metal truss bridge resting upon masonry piers.

6   A wooden bow-bridge with spile supports.

7   A segmental arch of wooden trusses with masonry abutments.

8   A wooden segmental arch with wooden abutments upon masonry piers.

9   A bow-bridge of wood, metal or masonry.

10   A segmental-arch type, of reinforced concrete upon masonry piers, or metal with masonry abutments.

11   Segmental-arch type built up of metal trusses and with lattice built up columns supporting the roadway.   Masonry pier foundations.

12   A segmental-arch type of metal plates and columns with ornamental approach of masonry.

13   A span bridge of metal trusses with masonry piers, the roadway supported by the lower curve of the segment.

14   The roadway supported by built up metal piers and spans, resting upon masonry shoes.

15   A combination of truss and span-bridge with metal members.

16   A combination of cantilever and truss bridges of metal.

17   A suspended bridge built of metal links.

18   A combination of cantilever and suspension.

19   A suspension bridge with masonry anchors and pylons.

20   A combination of suspension and span, with masonry anchors and piers and metal pylons.

21   Truss spans combined with a cantilever.

22   A suspension bridge with metal pylons and intermediate supports, between the masonry anchors and start of the span.

23   A suspension bridge with masonry anchors, pylons and piers.

24   A combination of suspension and swing bridge with masonry anchors and towers.

25   Showing the mechanical principle of the swing bridge, the roadway lifting vertically.

26   The swing bridge with one end rotating about a pivot.

27   The swing bridge with a pivoted center.

28   The swing bridge with a fixed end.

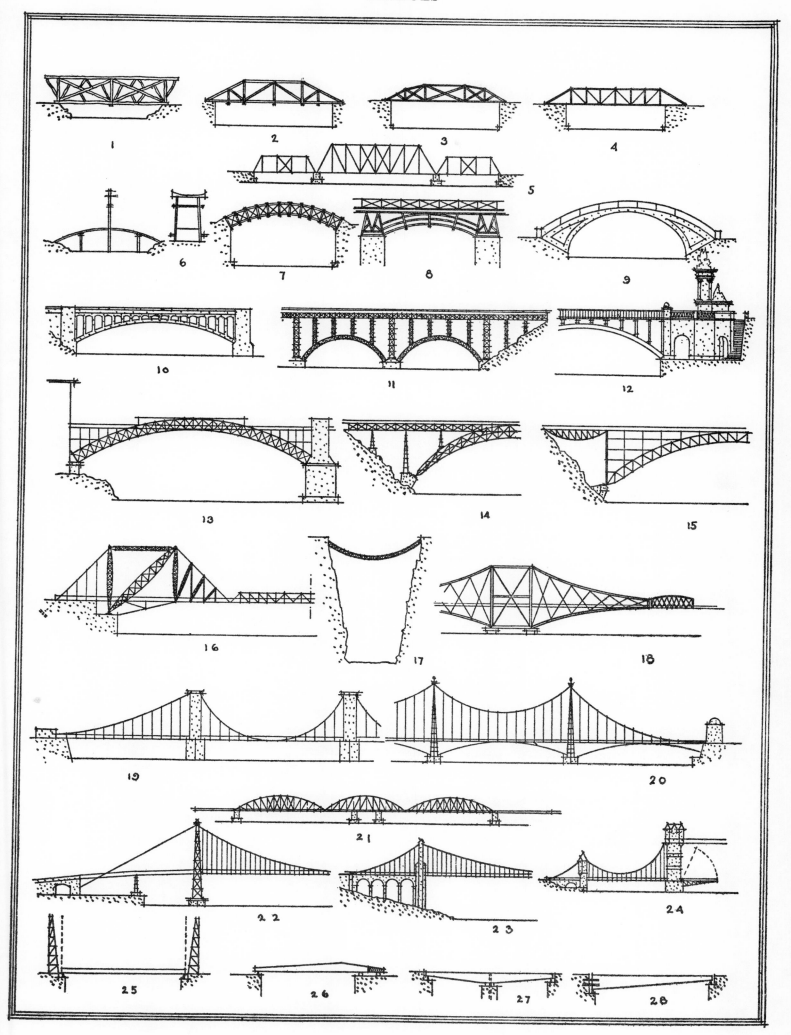

Plate 10

BUTTRESSES

The buttress is an abutment to a wall, and is used as a decoration or structurally, to increase the weight of a wall, and act as a reinforcement for loads and thrusts.

1 A simple buttress with slight projection.

2 A buttress in a wall with a batter. Orders, human figures, grotesques, etc., used.

3 An order with statuary used as a buttress.

4 Simple form of triangular buttress.

5 Elaboration of No. 4.

6 A triangular buttress and a plain buttress in combination with a chamfer.

7 A buttress elaborated with a base, niche and orders.

8 Superimposed buttresses with diminishing masses.

9 A simple buttress with increasing mass.

10 Corner buttresses placed at right angles to each other.

11 A simple sloping buttress with a canopy termination.

12 A corner buttress placed at an angle.

13 A buttress of great projection with a canopy termination and a doorway in the wall.

14 A free standing buttress receiving the thrust from another by a masonry arch, called a flying buttress. The outer buttress is weighted by increased height.

15 A buttress with great projection, pierced with an opening the head of which carries the resultant thrust.

16 A buttress and tower in combination.

17 A flying buttress with massive base.

18 A double flying buttress.

19 A double flying buttress with elaborated outer buttress.

20 A double flying buttress with lateral buttresses on the outer one.

21 Double flying buttresses with two outer buttresses.

22 Double flying buttresses with two outer buttresses, showing the relation to the roof, nave and side aisles.

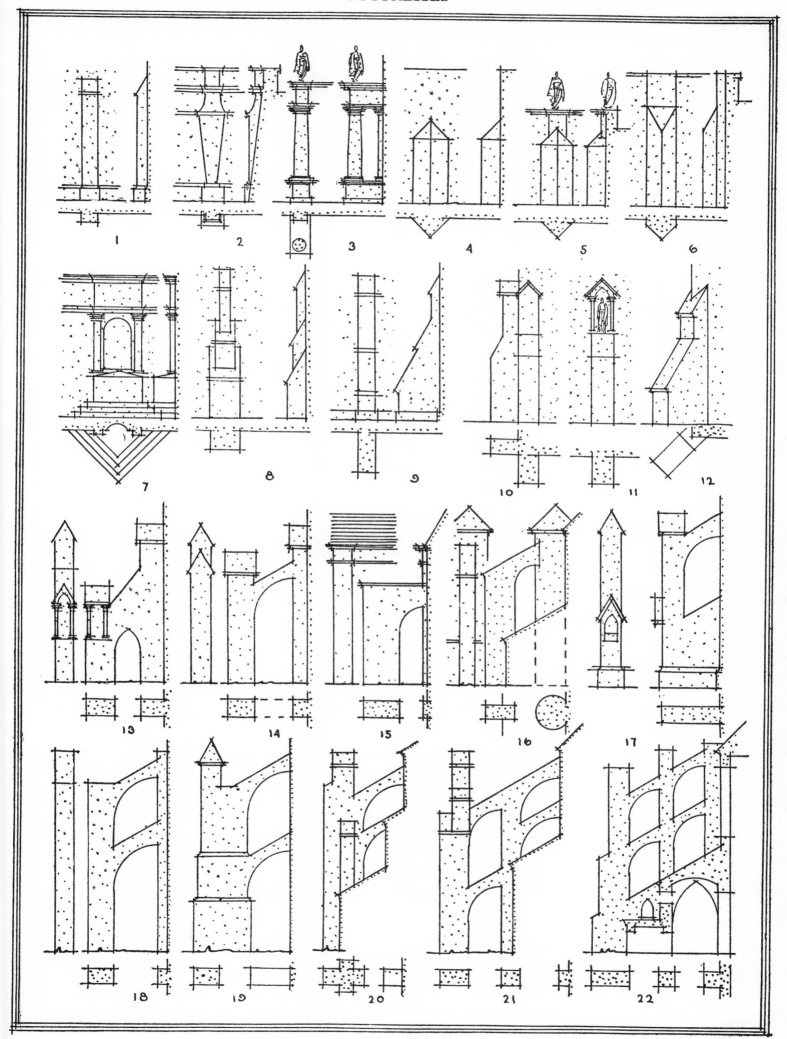

Plate 11

CEILINGS

The ceiling is a covering of the inner roof, and may have a flat, curved or combination of flat and curved surfaces. It may be self-supporting, hung or supported by beams.

1–2 The structural members exposed and decorated with polychrome and carving.

3 Structural members of a truss ornamented with carving.

4 An elaboration of the structural members with verticals and carving.

5 The use of wall brackets and caissons.

6 Ceiling beams with painted ornamentation.

7 A ceiling supported upon girders and beams, with or without polychrome embellishment.

8–9 Girders and beams with built-up panel motives between.

10 A border of panels with a central diamond shaped panel.

11 Circular central motives, with side paneling.

12 Irregularly shaped border-panels with an elaborated central motive.

13 Painted medallions, arabesques and bands.   Flat or in relief.

14 Examples with diamond shaped central panels and circular and rectangular outer panel motives.

15 Motives with a cruciform central panel and variously shaped side and border panels.

16 Border motives with square central panels subdivided.

17 Grouped panel compositions, the panels having various outlines.

18 Examples of a star-shaped central motive with side paneling.

19 A central diamond-shaped panel within a rhombus.

20 A circular central motive within a rhombus.

21 A ceiling of panels with alternating motives.

22 A ceiling with square and oblong panels.

23 A repeating motive having a square with outer panels.

24 Paneling formed by squares spaced equidistant and with their outer corners connected.

25 Paneling formed by hexagons and triangles.

26 Cruciform and octagonal motives in combination.

27 A composition with six-pointed star panels with their points in contact with one another.

28 Paneling with hexagonal, triangular and parallelogram motives.

29 Paneling with the square and diamond motive.

30 The circle, octagon and square in combination.

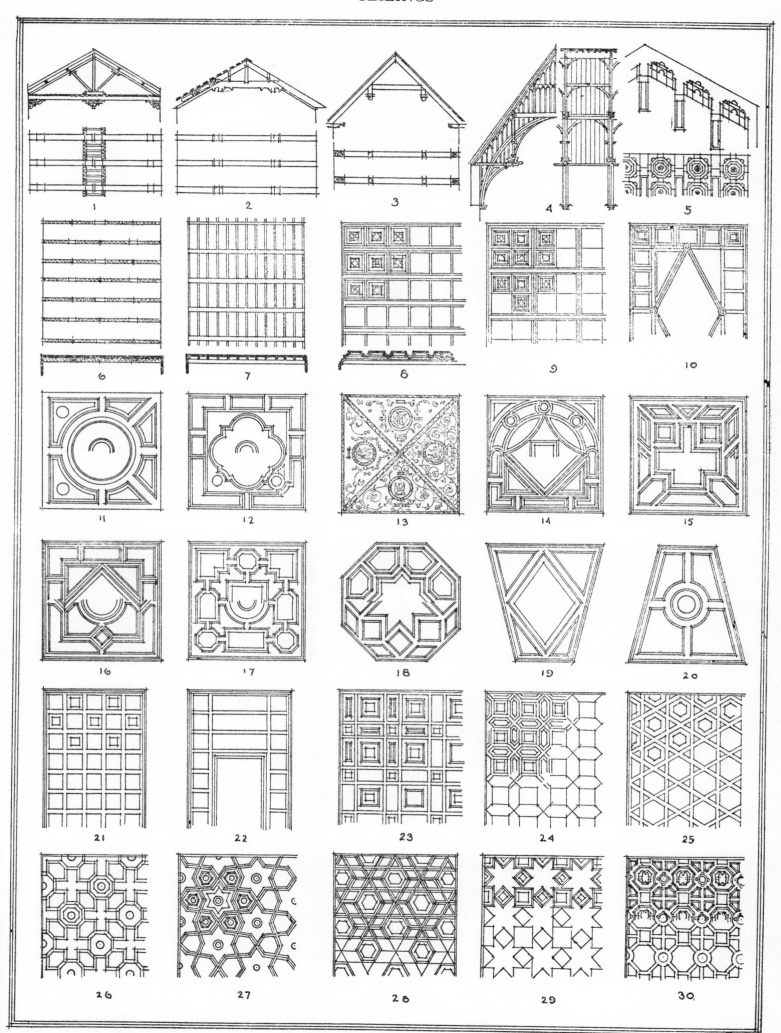

Plate 12

CEILINGS

Dealing with coved and composite surfaces

1 Examples with coves at the sides and embellishment at the miters, and a large central panel motive.

2 A sloping cove treated with panels, also with consoles or brackets.

3 A coved ceiling with penetrations embellished with panels and polychrome.

4 A curved ceiling with ribs in a motive and painted ornamentation within the divisions. Brackets and pendents used as further enrichment.

5 A curved ceiling with a diaper motive of circles and diagonals.

6 A curved ceiling with a diaper of intersecting circles.

7 A curved ceiling with a motive of tangent circles, also a motive with a compound-curve, circle and square.

8 A curved ceiling with a circle and a square in combination, also an example of a circle and star shaped motive.

9 A barrel vault with sunken caissons.

10 A barrel vault with penetrations with embellishment along the intersections and lateral bands.

11 A barrel vault embellished with parallel panels.

12 A barrel vault with penetrations and panels.

13 Domed ceilings with polychrome motives.

14 A domed ceiling and cupola with a painted architectural composition.

15 Domed ceilings treated with coffers and mosaic.

16 A double dome ornamented with panels in polychrome and modeled motives in high relief.

17 A domed ceiling with a central octagonal panel and eight side panels, the dividing members in relief and the panels filled with painting.

18 A vaulted ceiling with painted or modeled motives enclosed within the triangles formed by the groins.

19 A groined ceiling with painted motives.

20 A ceiling with a ribbed vault with cross and diagonal ribs.

21 Pyramidal vaulted ceiling with carved members.

22 A conoidal vaulted ceiling with carved members.

23 A domical ceiling upon pendentives, with carved ornamentation.

24 A ceiling with beams and stalactite carving.

25 A stalactite pendentive.

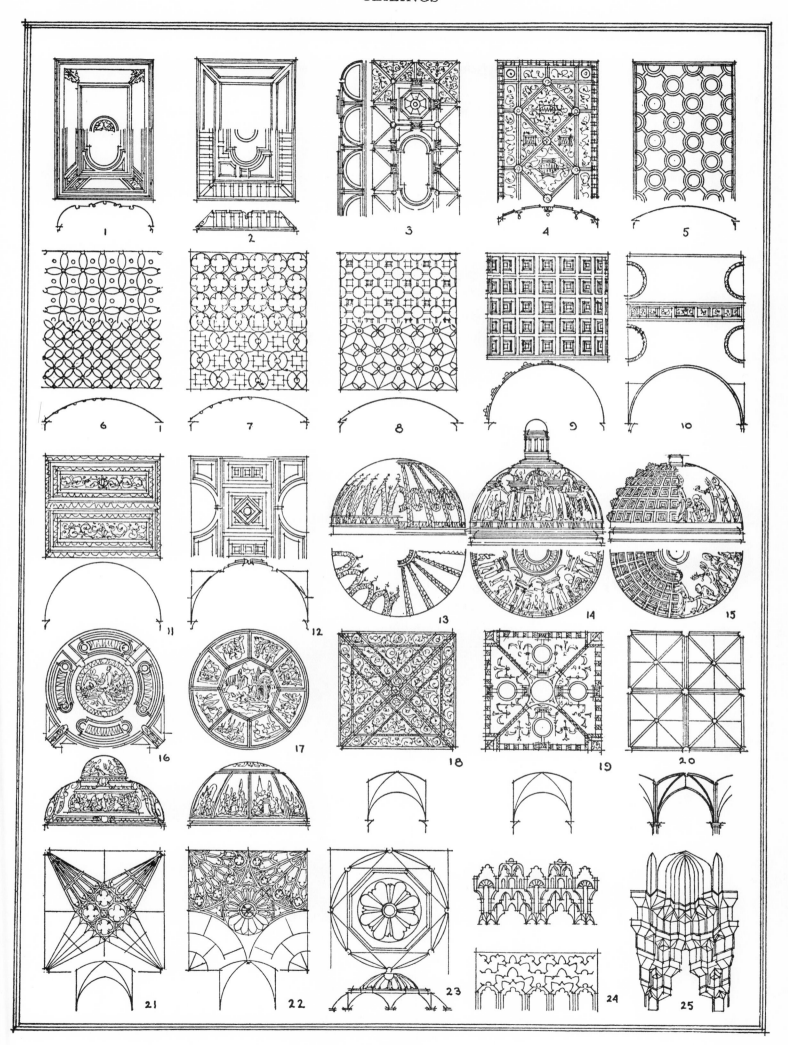

Plate 13

CHIMNEYS

The chimney comprises the structural treatment of the opening and passage through which smoke ascends.

1 At the end or side of a building, a chimney with a base reinforcement treated as a bay.

2 Stepped motive at the end of a building.

3–4 Buttress motive on the side and at the end of a building.

5–6–7–8–9 Various types of chimneys.

10–11 Examples of receding brick courses forming sloping sides.

12 A chimney with a flue in the wall and with a reinforced projecting base.

13 An irregular composition.

14 A symmetrical buttress motive.

15 A buttress motive with a gable and featured termination.

16 A chimney emerging from the roof ridge.

17 The wall continued above the roof, forming the chimney.

18 An end elevation of No. 17.

19 A chimney with a different motive for the upper part.

20 A chimney placed at the corner of a building.

21 A crude type of chimney supported by a wall bracket.

22–23–24 Wall chimneys supported upon brackets.

25 A wall chimney supported upon corbels and extending through a projecting gable.

26 A chimney at the top of an end gable.

27 The top member of a stepped gable serving as a chimney.

28 A chimney placed on the side of an end gable.

29 Coupled terminations at the apex of a gable.

30 Chimney terminations at the sides of a gable.

31 Coupled chimneys at the center of a gable end.

32 A chimney incorporated in a crenelated parapet.

33 A chimney resting upon corbels at the apex of a gable.

TERMINATIONS

34 Small brick vaults over flues as a weather protection.

35 A masonry slab with corner supports.

36 A dissymmetrical terra cotta termination.

37 Pentagonal terminations in a pyramidal cap.

38 Diamond shaped terminations in a pyramidal cap.

39 A group of circular terminations.

40 A group of octagonal terminations.

41 Ornamental columns as chimney terminations, astride a gabled cap.

42 Terra cotta pots used as a chimney termination.

43–44–45 Various masonry chimney tops with ornamental terra cotta terminations.

46–47–48 Terra cotta terminations with inner weather protection device.

49 A gabled cap with arched openings as a chimney termination.

50 An octagonal ornamental stack of terra cotta.

51 A chimney termination, emerging at the corner of a cornice and concealed within an ornamental composition.

52 A chimney terminating in an octagonal campanile.

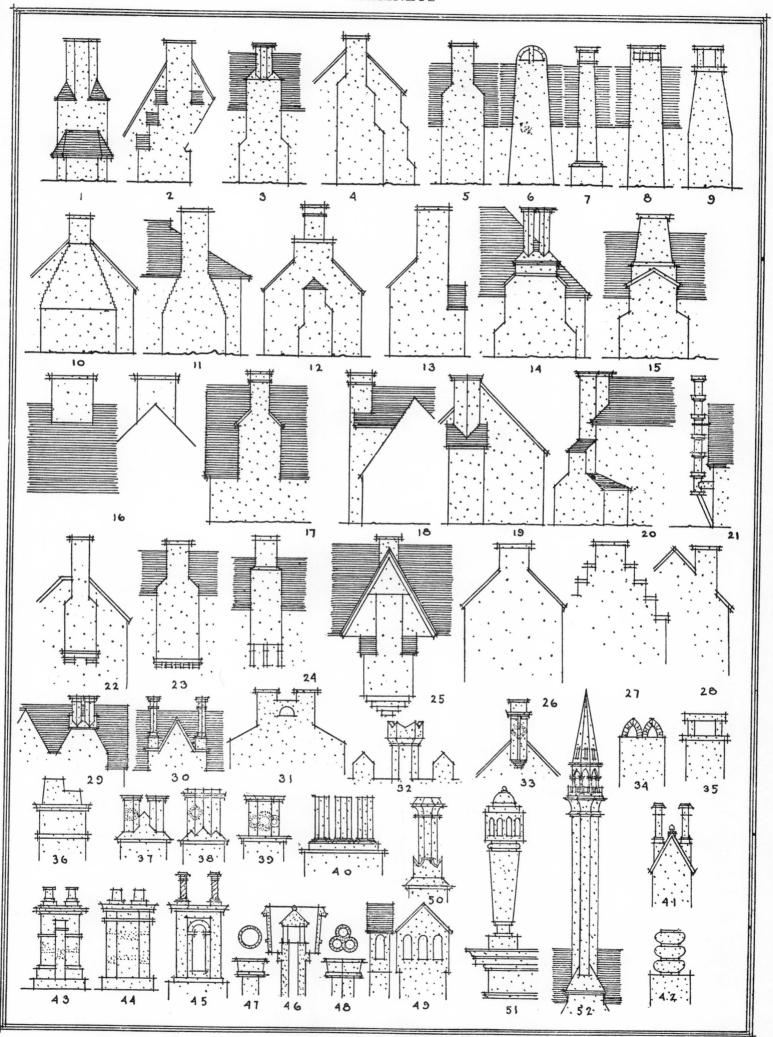

Plate 14

COLUMNS

The column is a round pillar or shaft, used singly or to support or adorn a building.

1   A free-standing column.

2   Two columns supporting an entablature.

3   A group of four columns, supporting an entablature and ornament.

4   Columns placed at the corners of a small edifice.

5   Columns grouped in a circular plan, supporting an entablature and dome.

6   Paired columns flanking a pedestal in a canopy motive.

7   Paired columns incorporated in the sides of a composition.

8   Ornamental columns flanking a statue in a stepped composition.

9   Columns used in a portico motive.

10   A column in an entrant angle.

11   A three-quarter engaged column in the corner of a wall.

12   Free standing columns at the corner of an edifice.

13   A column between two arches in a salient composition.

14   A free standing column supporting statuary in composition with a wall pilaster.

15   Columns in a projecting quadrant motive.

16   Columns in a semicircular plan grouping.

17   Paired columns at the inner sides of a doorway composition.

18   A column between two arches, a column supported upon a bracket overhead as ornamentation.

19–20   Columns at the inner sides of an opening.

21   Free standing columns flanking an opening.

22   Coupled columns in a colonnade and terminal motives.

23   Columns within an opening flanked with pilasters.

24   Free standing coupled columns in composition with a sub order motive.

25   Coupled columns within an entrance composition.

26   Engaged columns flanking a niche.

27   Engaged columns in a wall colonnade.

28–31   Engaged and free standing columns in an entrance motive.

29   Engaged columns in a colonnade composition between large masses.

30   Coupled columns and pilasters in a composition between large masses.

32   Columns within an opening and also flanking the opening.

33   Coupled columns and pilasters flanking an opening and also within the opening.

34   Engaged coupled columns with piers in a colonnade.

Plate 15

COLONNADES

The colonnade is a combination or grouping of columns arranged with regard to their structural or ornamental relation with a building.

1   A simple colonnade with a pier or column termination, in a single or double row of columns.

2   A colonnade around a pier or wall end.

3   A colonnade in front of a wall with pilasters along the wall corresponding to the columns.

4   A colonnade around an enclosure, double in front and single at the sides.

5   A colonnade around an enclosure, tripled in front and single at the sides.

6   A row of columns with a pier and three-quarter engaged column as a termination.

7   A double row of columns with a pier and three-quarter engaged column termination.

8   Examples of single and double colonnades terminating against piers.

9   A colonnade with wall piers, doubled and tripled.

10   A double colonnade portico motive in combination with a single one.

11   Various methods of grouping columns in a colonnade.

12   A colonnade with a projecting motive for special emphasis.

13   A central dominant colonnade reducing to a single one with a sub-order.

14   A semi-circular double colonnade with a central pavilion and pylon terminations.

15   A motive with statuary and columns.

16–18   Colonnades applied in front of an opening for emphasis.

17   A colonnade within an opening.

19   A colonnade with a sub-order screening a larger one.

20   A semi-circular colonnade with end terminations in combination with a row of columns in front of the terminations.

21   A single colonnade in combination with a sub-order and statuary.

22   A colonnade emphasized at the center by column grouping and projecting beyond the general mass.

23   Superimposed columns in groups of two and three in a colonnade.

24   Superimposed colonnades of various heights.

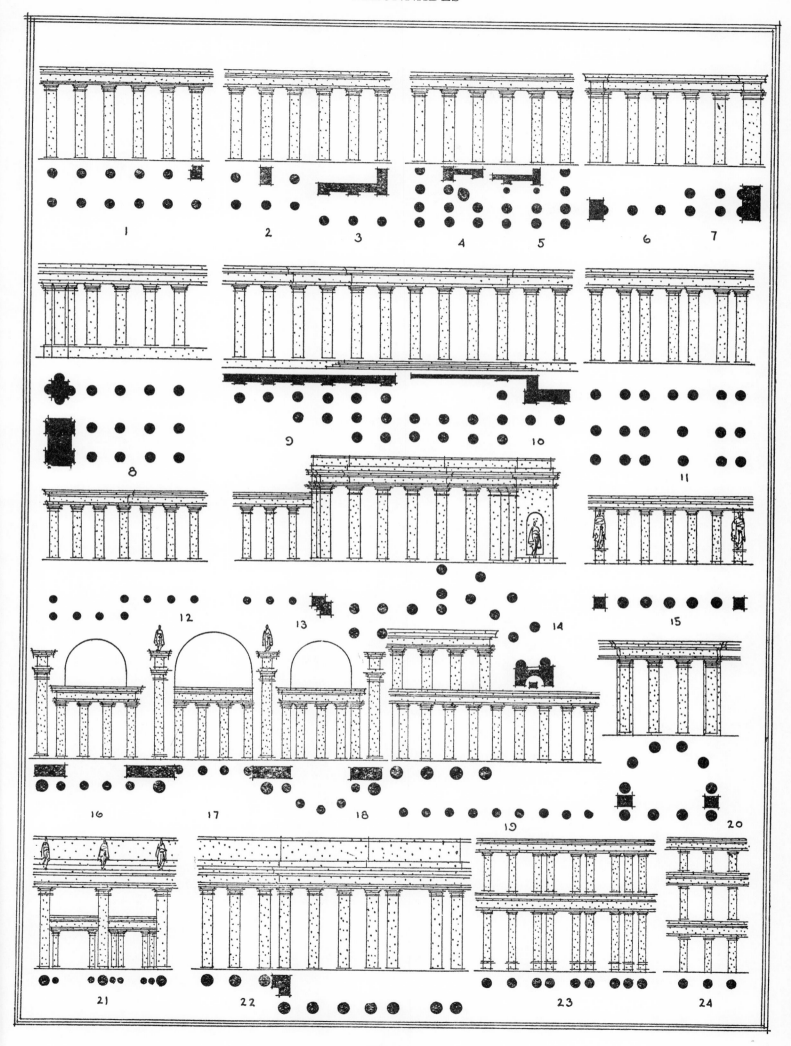

Plate 16

COURTS

The court is an open space about which a building or several buildings are grouped, completely or partially enclosing this space. They may be roofed or open to the air.

1–3   An outer court between wings.

2   An outer court between wings enclosed by a colonnade.

4   A court between buildings with an end loggia.

5–7   Courts formed in the entrant angle of two wings and enclosed with walls on the open sides.

6–10   Three wings forming two outer courts.

8   An approach obtained by the use of a monumental fore court.

9   Open and closed courts in combination with passages.

11–12   Central courts with one entrance.

13   A central court with small corner courts.

14   An open court within wings of varying heights.

15   A central court with two entrances and corner emphasis.

16   A central court with an arcade around the sides.

17   A grouping of four similar edifices about an arcaded court.

18   A group plan showing outer and inner courts.

19   An inner court with shelters at the ends.

20–25   A symmetrically arranged inner court with an unbalanced entrance.

21   A symmetrical enclosed court with entrant and end vestibules.

22–23–24   Symmetrical grouping of buildings about inner courts.

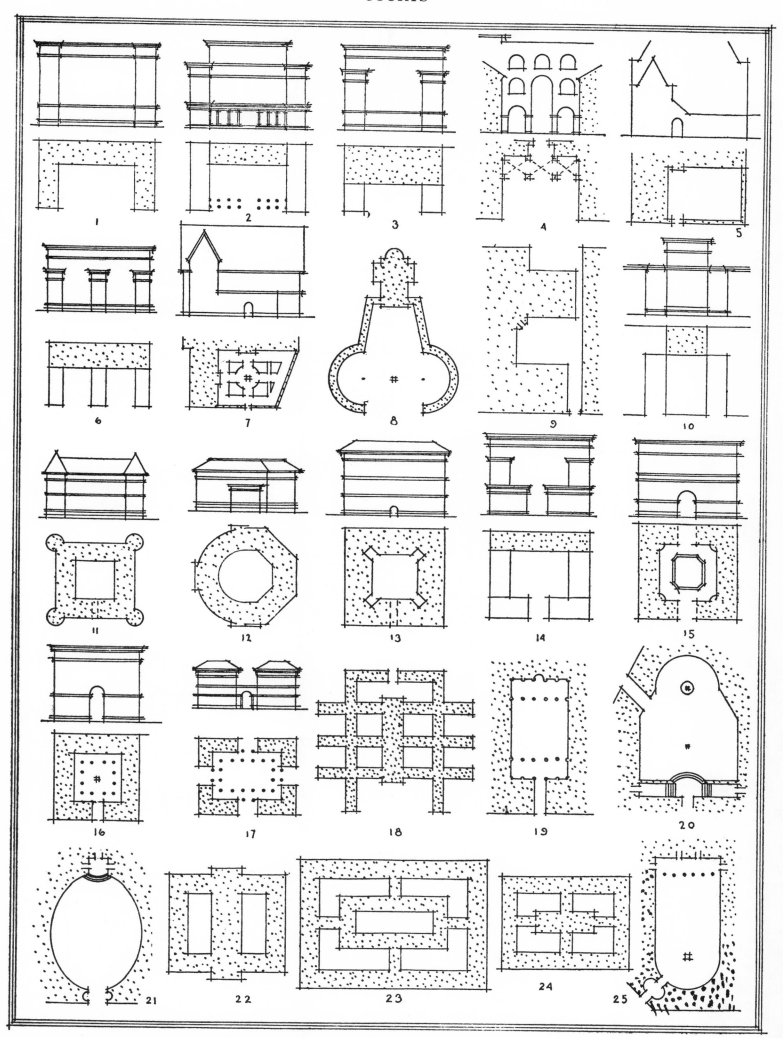

Plate 17

DOMES

The dome is a roof hemispherical in mass, or having an outline composed of simple or compound curves.

1 A conical covering above a circular plan, not a true dome but, the ceiling below is generally domical.

2 Similar to No. 1 but having an octagonal plan.

3 Superimposed conical roof coverings.   Not a true dome.

4 An octagonal spire-shaped roof covering.   Not a true dome.

5 A transition from the square to the octagon, the ceiling below is domical with hemispherical side-niches.

6 Similar to No. 1 but with the addition of a domed circular colonnade.

7 A stilted dome upon an octagonal drum.

8 An octagonal dome with concave sides.

9 A low dome with horizontal members at its base.

10 Similar to No. 9 but with a conical termination at the crown.

11 A dome composed of stepped bands and crowned with a domed cylindrical motive.

12–14 A dome with eight ribs and an ornamented crest.

13 A group of domes with compound curves.

15 A hemispherical dome and cupola composed of convex flutings.

16 A dome upon an arched octagon.

17 A stilted hemispherical dome crowned with one having a syma-recta curved outline.

18 A spherical dome with a circular arch composition at the sides.

19 A spherical dome crowned with a cylinder supporting another dome having a syma-recta curve in outline.

20 A dome upon cusped arches, crowned with a cylinder supporting a small dome whose outline is a cyma-recta.

21 A dome having a compound curve upon a square drum with chamfered corners.

22 A dome composed of hemispherical and conoidal masses upon an octagonal drum resting upon a square with chamfered corners.

23 Small low hemispherical domes in a composition flanking a larger central similar one upon a square drum with a termination at the crown having a compound curve.

24 A dome composed of hemispherical and conoidal masses supported upon a drum whose upper plan is a duodecagon and whose lower is an octagon. The whole resting upon a square.

25 A dome composed of hemispherical and conoidal masses, stilted and supported upon an octagonal drum.

26 A dome whose outline is a syma-reversa upon an octagon, crowned with a cupola having a similar covering.

27 A pointed dome whose outline is a segment of a circle upon a shallow drum resting upon an octagon chamfering into a square.

28 A shallow dome composed of conical and hemispherical masses resting upon a low drum with twenty sides, which is supported upon another low mass having eight sides.

29 A pointed dome whose outline is a segment of a circle, upon a duodecagonal drum with ornamental corner chamferings reducing it to a square.

30 A stilted hemispherical dome upon a shallow duodecagonal drum, crowned with an octagonal cupola with a pointed dome.

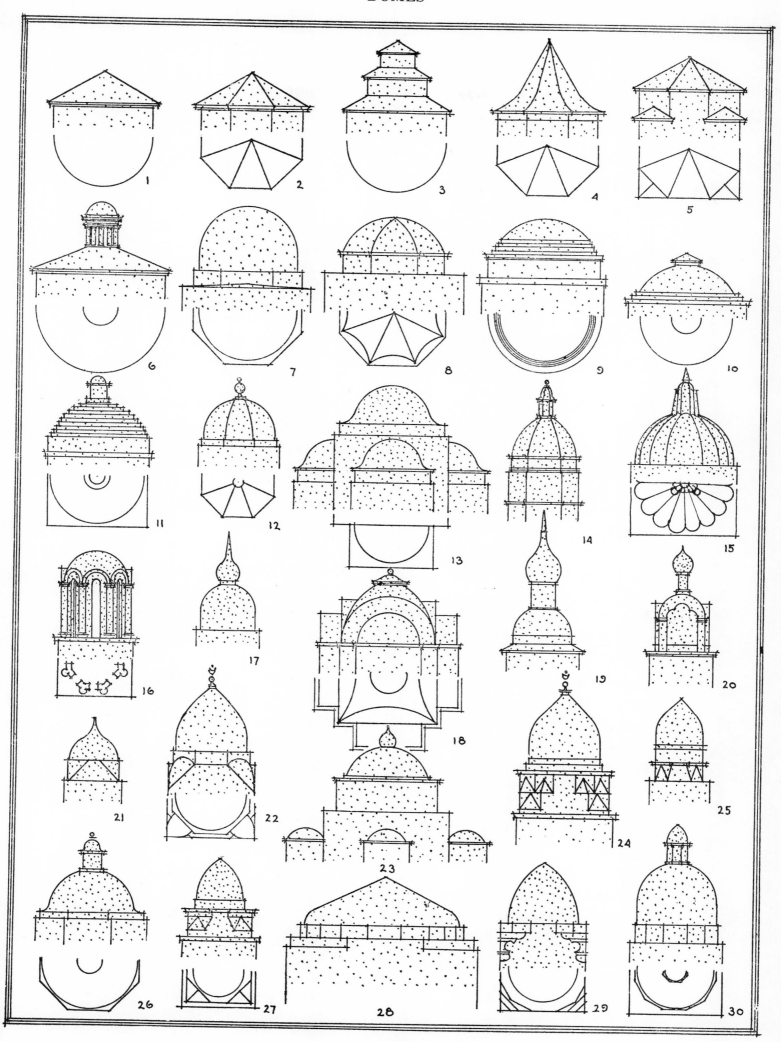

Plate 18

DOORWAYS

The doorway is an opening for entrance or exit to a building or a part, and includes such an opening and its intermediate surroundings.

1   A triangular shaped opening with corbeled sides.

2   An opening with a pointed head and voussoirs.

3   An opening with a circular head, head and spring of arch moulded.

4   Pointed head with grouped windows and moulding above.

5   Cusped head and pointed arch mouldings. Steps within the reveal.

6   A segmental head with a corbeled panel, or an opening overhead.

7   A pointed, arched head with piercings at the sides framed with a moulding. Steps within and without the reveal.

8   A circular headed opening with concentric reveals.

9   A circular headed opening with concentric reveals, elaborated.

10   Circular mouldings framing an arched opening with voussoirs in a pointed arch composition.

11   A pointed head with side reveals, within a gabled projecting motive.

12   Framed arcaded openings above an opening with splay sides and an arched head of compound curves.

13   An opening with a pointed arched piercing overhead, flanked with mouldings following the outline in a canopy motive.

14   An opening with a compound head within a circular headed reveal, flanked with columns.

15   An architraved circular headed opening, framed with flanking columns with an entablature and a base course.

16   An opening framed with a broken pediment upon columns and pedestals.

17   An arch supported by a column emphasizing an opening at an entrant angle of a wall.

18   An order with a curved pediment framing a circular headed opening.

19   Grouped orders flanking an opening, with a broken curved pediment.

20   Circular headed reveals within a pedimented motive.

21   A group of seven openings in a composition of canopied gables above pointed arched openings with stepped or recessed reveals.

22   Columns in the reveals of a circular headed doorway, with the outer columns embellished with entablatures and statuary.

23   An architraved opening within a frame supporting a pediment, keystones, and panels.

24   Grouped openings within a broken pediment motive supported upon columns flanking a doorway.

25–27   An opening flanked with columns supporting a vaulted canopy.

26   A balcony supported by orders flanking an opening.

28   Coupled openings with recessed reveals within a larger pointed arched opening with flanking columns.

29   A doorway with coupled openings above, in a composition having flanking columns, entablature and stilted pediment motive.

Plate 19

DOORWAYS

Dealing mostly with the square headed opening

1　An opening divided by a transom bar.

2　A framed opening with a semicircular one above.

3　A segmental arch with splayed sides, about an opening.

4　An opening with chamfered sides and head with arched overhead embellishment.

5　A framed opening with ornamented head and applied projecting pediment.

6　An opening with an architrave and cornice, with a circular headed opening or panel above.

7　An opening with an architrave and cornice and an overhead panel.

8　An opening with a pediment above supported upon consoles.

9–10　Openings with an architrave frame, frieze and pediment above.

11　An opening with mullions and transom motive enclosed in an architrave with frieze and cornice above.

12　A small opening above a doorway having a similar motive in a composition with architrave, frieze and cornice, consoles and festoons.

13　A doorway at the corner of a wall, with flanking columns and a hood motive.

14　An opening in a projecting frame with a broken circular pediment.

15　Doorway in an entrant angle with a side column and canopy motive.

16　A doorway within a triangular portico.

17　Consoles flanking a doorway and supporting a circular pediment, with an opening or a panel, and carving in the center.

18　A pedimented doorway with diagonal side members and consoles.

19–20　Examples of sculpture and pediments in combination over a doorway.

21　An architrave, frieze and cornice motive, with engaged columns in the door reveal and an overhead panel.

22　A pedimented order enclosing a doorway.

23　An architrave about an opening with sloping sides.

24　A doorway flanked with columns supporting a lintel.

25　Pier groups flanking a doorway, with consoles and a broken curved pediment having a central ornament.

26　Columns flanking a doorway, with a curved pediment motive.

27　A two storied motive with orders flanking the openings.

28　Coupled openings within a three columned pedimented portico, with statuary emphasizing the ends and a canopy of columns and pediment over the center.

29　Coupled central openings flanked with side openings in a composition of engaged columns, entablatures and arched mouldings.

30　A two storied motive with columns supporting a broken pediment, and a sub-order dividing the opening in two.

31　A two storied motive of superimposed column and pediment compositions.

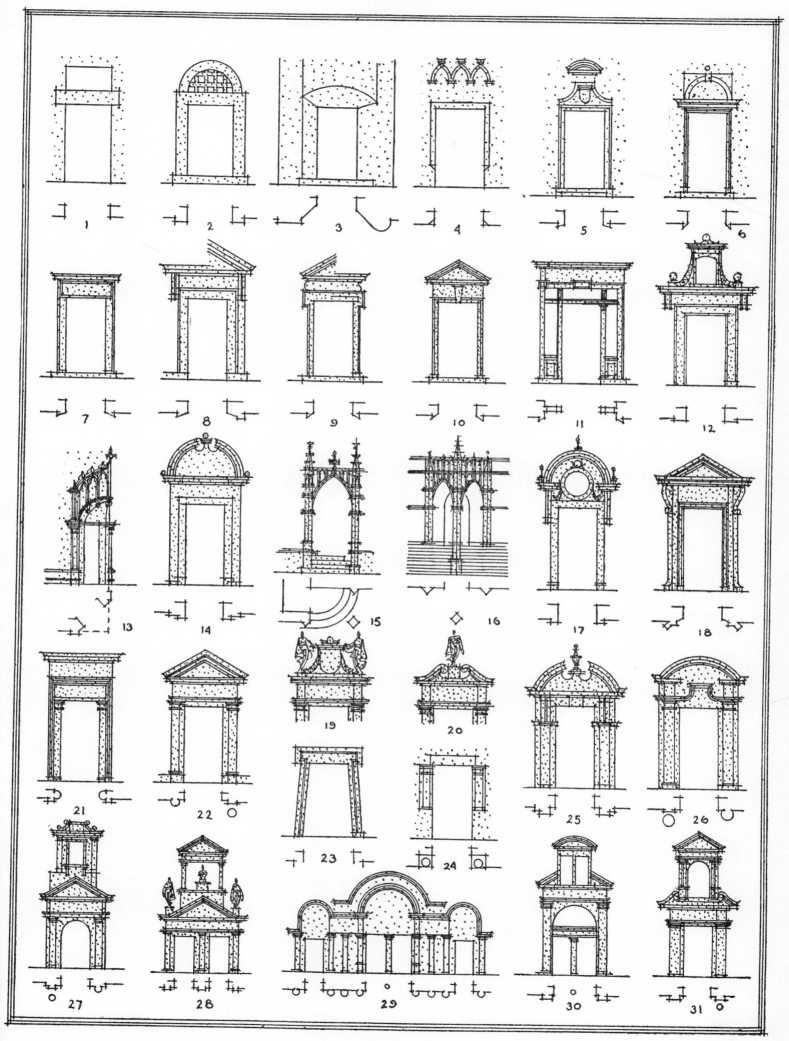

Plate 20

DORMERS

The dormer is a window pierced vertically in the slope of the roof, or combined with a gabled extension of the wall of the building and the roof.

1   A vertical opening cut in the side wall and roof slope.

2   An opening in the side wall and roof slope, with head and sides framed into the roof.

3–6   Side walls projecting above the eaves and roofed with a ridge roof.

4   A dormer with a hipped roof framed into a chimney at the side.

5   A dormer with a hipped roof framed between chimneys.

7   Superimposed dormers.

8   The side wall forming the dormer with a single slope roof.

9   A dormer with a jerkin headed roof.

10   A dormer with a hipped roof.

11   A dormer with a horizontal accent with a single slope roof.

12   A dormer with twin gables.

13   A horizontal dormer motive with gabled dormers at the ends.

14   A gable roofed with the projecting upper slope of a gambrel roof.

15   Similar to No. 14 but with side hips to the roof.

16   A horizontal dormer along the ridge of a roof.

17   A dormer with an architrave and pediment.

18   A dormer with side consoles supporting a circular pediment.

19   A circular headed dormer.

20   An eyebrow dormer with a sloping roof.

21   An opening in the wall and roof having a semicircular conical ridge roof.

22   An octagonal dormer with a spire.

23   A dormer with a ridge roof projecting forward, serving as a hood.

24–26   Pedimented colonnades forming a dormer motive.

25   A Palladian motive dormer composition.

27   An arched dormer in a tower spire.

28   A gabled dormer with a balcony and half-timber construction.

29   Superimposed independent gables in a roof slope.

30   An opening in the roof slope with an octagonal spire serving for a hood.

31   An elaborated dormer with coupled openings, columns, entablature and a gable with compound curves.

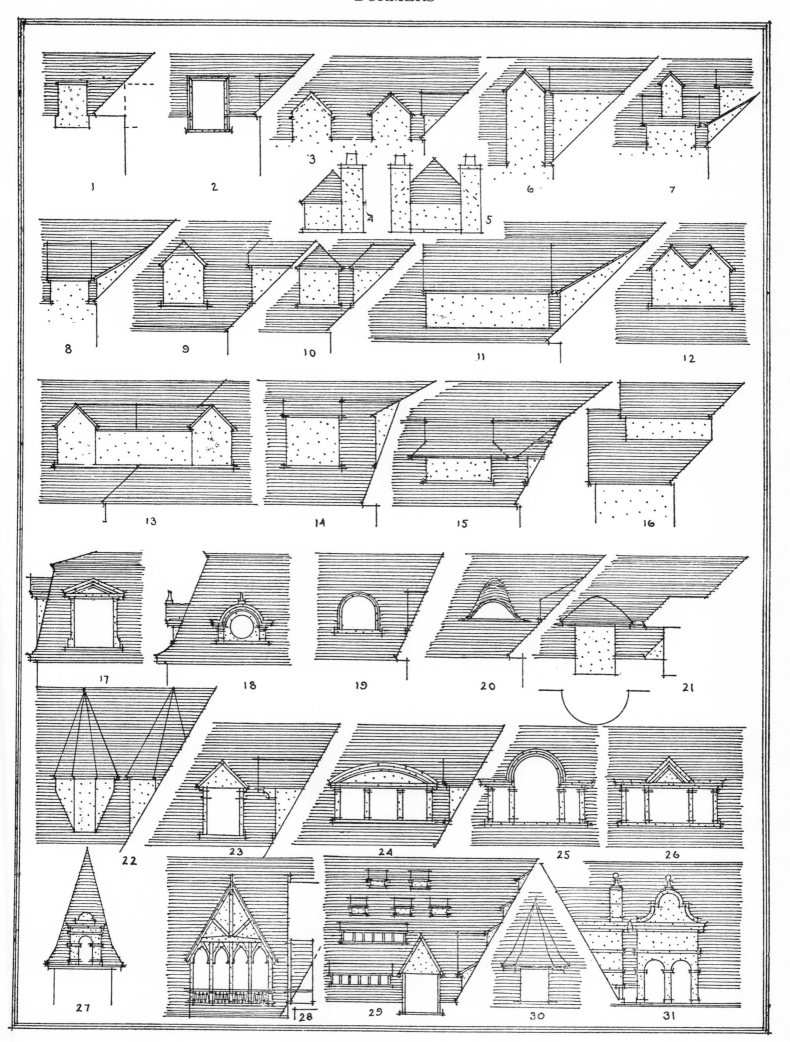

Plate 21

FACADES

The facade is the architectural front of a building.

Dealing with examples emphasizing the center of the composition

1 A projecting entrance-composition, half the facade height.

2 A projecting central mass exceeding the sides in height and with a transitional treatment uniting the difference in levels.

3–5 A projecting entrance-composition of one story.

4 A projecting central motive with twin gables.

6 Excessive height and roof embellishment emphasizing the center.

7 Greater height, mass and embellishment at the entrance and of the roof emphasizing the facade.

8 A pedimented portico at the center of a simple composition.

9 A portico with an attic, in the center of a simple composition.

10–24 A projecting central composition of greater height and more important roof treatment.

11 The central projecting mass terminated with a pediment and an increase of height by the use of a drum, dome and cupola, emphasizing the center of the whole composition.

12 A projecting mass at the center of a composition in combination with another projecting central mass with a pediment.

13 A salient mass at the center in combination with a tower.

14 A chimney and gabled wing motive in a center emphasis composition.

15–21 The central salient projecting above the facade in a tower composition.

16 A colonnade motive, with the central feature a pedimented portico with an order of greater height.

17 An order and attic motive, with the central feature a pedimented portico with further central emphasis from a drum and dome.

18 Projecting pylons enclosing a colonnade as a central feature.

19 A flight of steps and a central portico as an emphasis at the center.

20 A pedimented portico, with a drum and dome emphasizing the mass.

22 A central mass with excessive height and double projecting motives.

23 A flight of steps, a portico and a roof pediment featuring a composition for central expression.

25 A one-storied colonnade between a two-storied pylon motive in a composition for central emphasis.

26 Receding superimposed masses, with slim towers flanking the center leading to a crowning dome.

27 A pedimented projecting feature of superimposed colonnades.

28 Coupled orders with sculpture in a gabled mass composition.

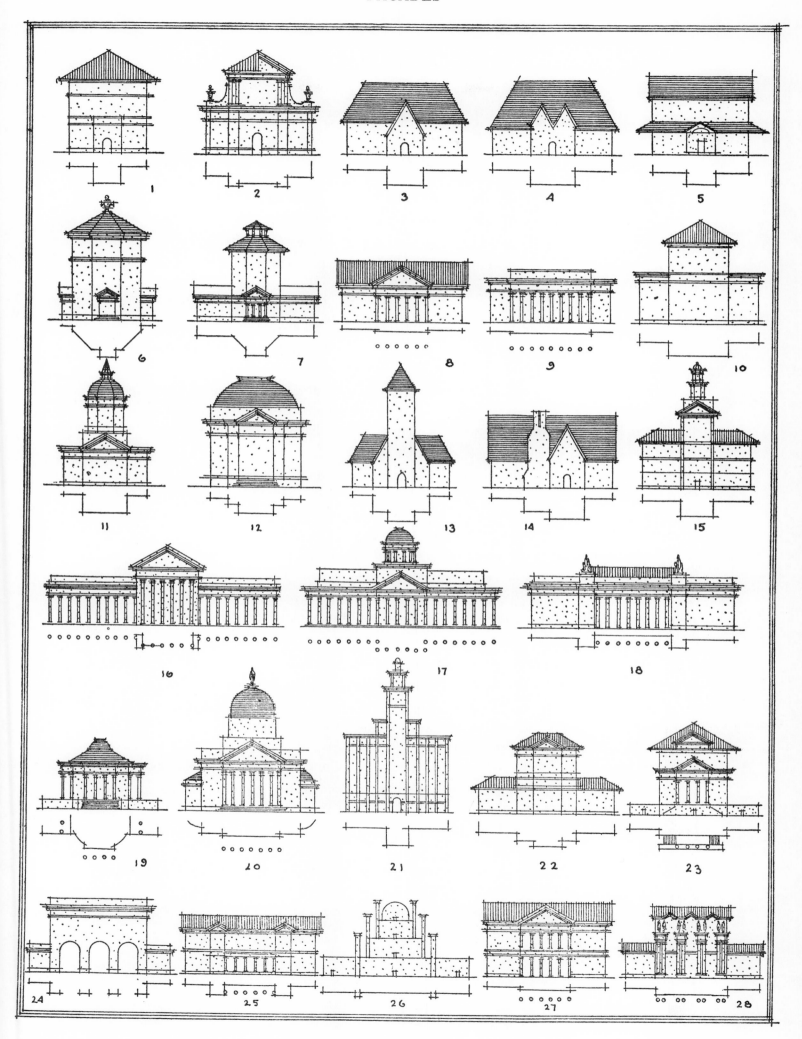

Plate 22

FACADES

Dealing with central and end emphasis

1 Salient features the whole composition height, at the center and ends.

2 A central salient of repeated motives and end rustication.

3 End wings in composition with a central roof mass of greater height.

4 End salients the total height of the composition with a central projecting feature of half the total height.

5 A central doorway in a plain mass with domes at the ends.

6 End salient features with a central pedimented portico.

7 Salient features at the ends and center, which is further emphasized by a pediment and tower motive.

8 A central tower with flanking smaller ones in an octagonal composition of superimposed horizontals.

9 End tower motives, with a central mass of equal height and superimposed porticos.

10 End towers and a central one of greater height.

11 End salients with an order, flanking a mass with this order at a higher level, with a high central spire.

12 A facade divided into three bays with projecting buttresses, the central mass greater in height to balance the heavier end buttresses.

13 A composition with end towers and a greater central one.

14 A facade with end towers and a central roof-spire.

15 Pylons at the ends of an arcade composition, with a greater central one in an entrance motive. Additional central emphasis is obtained by a great central tower-like mass.

16 End salients with dormer note, and a central salient of greater height, with a pediment.

17 Central and end tower motives, the central composition of greater height and importance.

18 End salients with pediments and a central mass of greater height with a dome.

19 End and central salients of equal height, but greater projection and mass with a drum and dome, completes the dominance of the central composition.

20 A composition in which the central mass is treated with end porticos, and the center with a dominant salient with coupled columns at the corners and an arched pediment.

21 End and central tower motives, with superimposed orders at the ends and a portico with a drum with orders and dome overhead.

22 A composition with five salients in tower motives. One at the ends and three, in a central composition.

23 A composition with six salient features. One at each end and four massed in a central motive, of which the two inner salients have a different plan for particular emphasis.

24 A composition with four sadients. One at each end and one at the ends of a central salient, with an attic and dome.

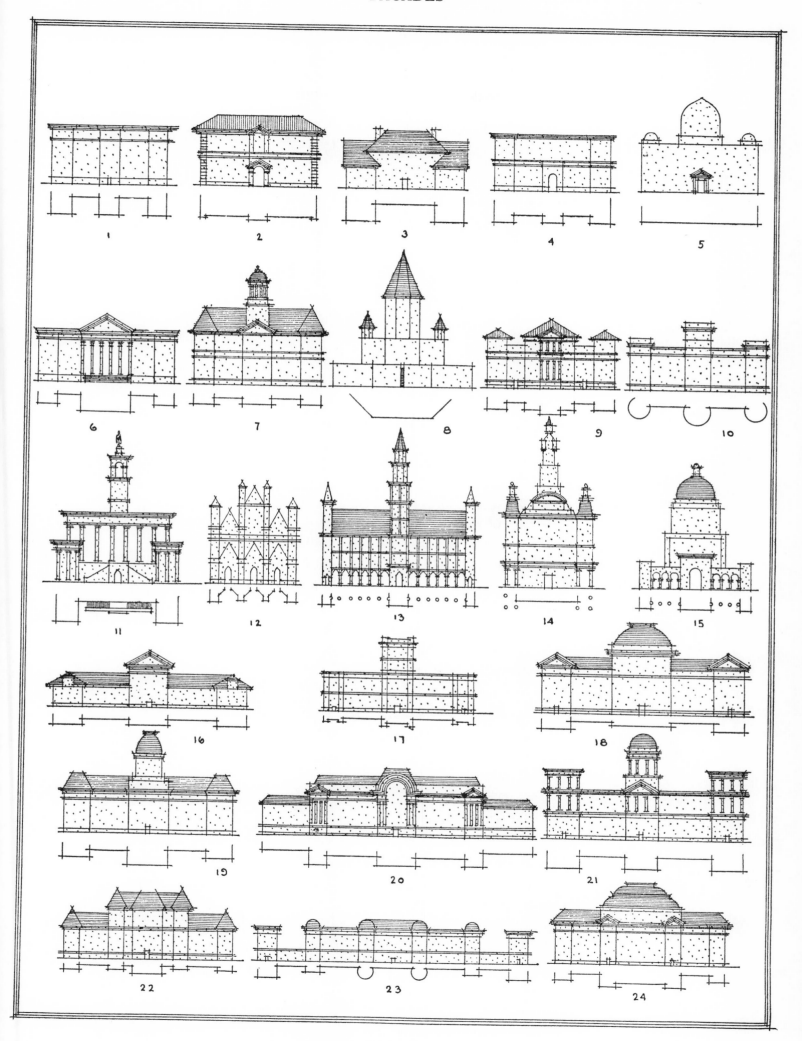

Plate 23

FACADES

Dealing with horizontal emphasis and vertical emphasis

1 A flat surfaced composition with belt courses and cornice.

2 Receding superimposed horizontal masses.

3 An arcade, belt courses, low roof and cornice in a horizontal composition.

4–15 Base, belt courses and terminating arcades, in a horizontal composition.

5 Base, colonnade, entablature and terminating colonnades in a composition emphasizing the horizontal.

6 Low roof, belt course and elongated quoins, in a horizontal composition.

7–16 Superimposed belt courses and a cornice, in a composition with a decided horizontal note.

8 A simple oblong mass with cornice and a central spire, with the feeling of the oblong dominant.

9 A horizontal mass with a circular colonnade above, supporting a smaller domed circular colonnade.

10 A flat mass with cornice, and a horizontal opening in the upper part with a colonnade therein, making a horizontal note.

11 Colonnades used in a facade at the base and top, in a horizontal composition.

12–14 Superimposed coupled columns, with their entablatures, the whole composition having a horizontal emphasis.

13 Superimposed orders in a "Screen Front" motive with a horizontal note.

17 Roofs and belt courses in a composition with a horizontal note.

18–19–20 Colonnade compositions in which the mass is conflicting with the vertical note of the ornamental motives.

21 A vertical composition of parallel panel openings.

22 A vertical composition of corner piers and central openings divided into vertical parts.

23 A flat composition with parallel vertical openings, giving a decided vertical note.

24 Superimposed arches in a gabled composition, with a vertical note produced by emphasizing the structural lines of the composition.

25–27 An arcade at the base of a composition with the columns determining the divisioning of the facade, producing a vertical note.

26 Parallel voids in a gable composition, producing a vertical expression.

28 A gabled composition in half timber. The structural expression is obviously vertical.

29 A composition with buttressed pier divisions, and window mullions extending through several stories. Decidedly vertical in expression.

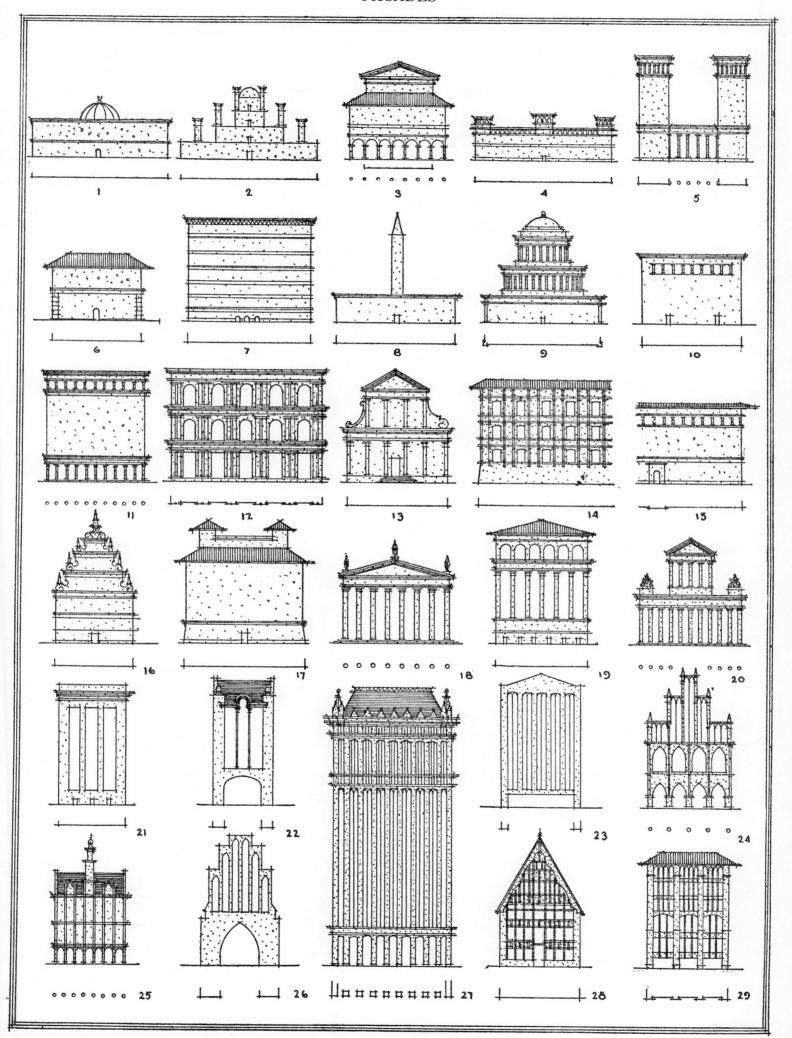

Plate 24

FACADES

Dealing with end emphasis and also dissymmetric compositions

1 End salients with double projections and porticos with pediments.

2 End salients of great projection and pedimented.

3 End wings with stepped roof terminations.

4 End salients with roof treatment for an emphasis note.

5 An arcade composition with salient tower motives at the ends.

6 A composition with circular corner towers, dominating the facade.

7 A composition with corner turrets.

8 A dominant mass with circular corner towers.

9 A composition with diagonal end wings.

10 End wings in a composition with the same gable roof.

11–15 An arcade between end pylons.

12 Towers at the ends of a buttress composition.

13 Attenuated, superimposed towers at the ends of a horizontal mass.

14 High towers at the sides of a gable composition, flanking an apse end.

16 An "L" shaped gabled composition.

17 A gabled composition with smaller similar ones at one side.

18 A mass with a salient feature near one end, and with a similar but greater feature near the other.

19 A mass with a tower near one end.

20 A mass with a tower near one end, and a small similar mass on the other end.

21 A horizontal mass with a tower at one corner.

22 A mass with coupled gabled salients at one end, and an echo of the main mass at the other.

23 A gabled mass with a smaller repetition at the end. A spire near one end of the main mass.

24 The wall of a composition extending up in the form of a large gable at one end, twin dormer gables added for the sake of balance.

25 A gabled mass with a central salient feature and an applied side tower motive.

26 A composition of a small and large mass, with a small end salient balancing the smaller mass.

27 A gable composition with a corner tourelle and side wall.

28 A composition with a hip roof and tower in combination with a smaller roofed mass with corner tower.

29 A gabled mass composition with semi octagonal end, portal and belfry.

30 A mass with a salient feature at one side, with an additional projecting member as an entrance motive.

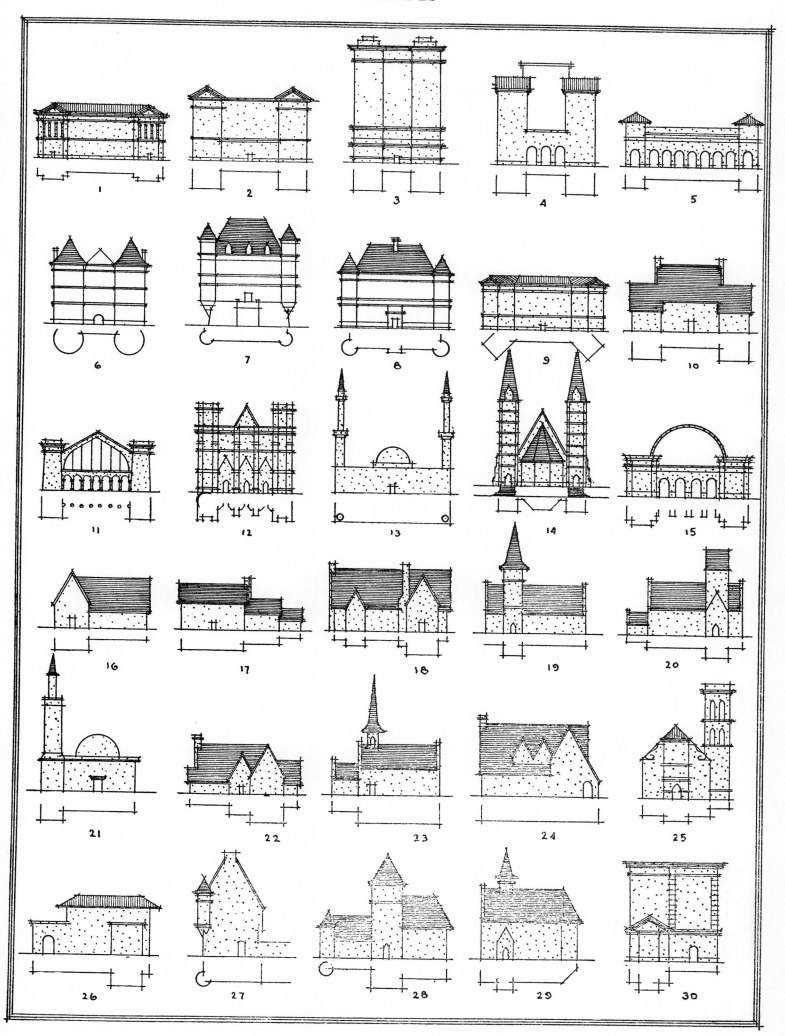

Plate 25

FIREPLACES

The fireplace is that part of a building which is arranged for the making of fires with relation to heating and cooking.

1   A central hearth in a chamber with an overhead smoke outlet.

2–4   Wall hearths with hoods above supported upon brackets.

3–7–9   Wall hearths flanked with columns supporting hoods.

5–6–10   Wall hearths with hoods supported upon various types of piers.

8   A fireplace with a segmental head and an opening above.

11–12   Wall hearths with hoods supported upon side brackets.

13–14–15   Various examples of hooded corner hearths.

16–22   Fireplaces framed with architraves.

17   Projecting bands parallel to the fireplace opening.

18   A fireplace within splays framed with an architrave.

19   A raised hearth with recessed bands around a segmental arched opening.

20–29–31–36   Fireplaces within recesses.

21   A stepped receding chimney breast serving as shelves.

23   A composition with flanking niches and an overhead panel.

24   A hooded fireplace within an arch.

25   Recessed reveals with overhead panels.

26   An architrave framing a fireplace with a pedimented panel above.

27   Superimposed orders in a mantel and overmantel composition.

28   A fireplace flanked with pilasters and having superimposed panels above.

30   A fireplace with an architrave around the opening and with a circular headed entablature supported upon consoles as an overmantel.

32–33   Architrave, frieze and cornice motives, with mantel shelf.

34   Caryatids flanking an opening and supporting the mantel shelf.

35   Consoles flanking an architrave, supporting a bracketed frieze and cornice composition.

Plate 26

FOUNTAINS

The fountain is an architectural setting, more or less elaborate, incorporating a continuous natural or artificial water supply.

1 A basin receiving water from an elevated free-standing ornament.

2 Water jets emerging from the sides of a shaft into a basin.

3 A central jet discharging into superimposed lower basins.

4 A dominant statuary group above receiving basins.

5 A central jet above superimposed receiving basins.

6 A central shaft with side jets flowing into superimposed basins.

7 Receding superimposed receiving basins supported upon carved ornaments, with a central water-jet in a cascade motive.

8 A fountain set in a pool, fronting an architectural feature.

9 A Kiosk with side jets and a receiving basin.

10 An architectural composition of niches and statuary, with side receiving basins over a large lower one.

11 The parapet of a stair enclosing a pool, the supply issuing from a pedestal on the stair landing.

12 A figure at the center of a tank, receiving water jets from the ends of the pool.

13 A combination of the "Statuary Group Motive," and the "Pool and jet Motive."

14 A "Tank Motive" with a basin and central jet at one end and a central stepped channel overflow.

15 A "Cascade Motive" with the source at the base of a piece of sculpture, descending with repeated motives into a lower pool.

16 A circular pool and central jet on an upper level, in combination with a lower pool, connected by cascades.

17 An "Architectural Composition" at the head of a pool, which emerges as a cascade flowing into a receiving pool below.

18 A "Chateau d'Eaux" motive, composed of parapets, niches, sculpture and descending cascades with a receiving pool on one side of an avenue; and stairs flanking a pool with cascades and wall jets, on the other side.

19 Roadways connecting upper and lower pools in an ornamental motive of jets, pools and cascades.

20 An octagonal pool, with side channels, placed in front of a temple motive. Water jets, recessed in the sides of the channels, providing the supply.

Plate 27

FOUNTAINS

Dealing with the well-head and the wall fountain

1 An antique column capital upon steps serving as a well-head.

2 An octagonal mass upon octagonal steps, serving as a well-head.

3 A column capital upon a circular slab with metal frame above.

4 A pedestal motive with metal frame above.

5 A circular well-head upon a circular slab with flanking columns and architrave.

6 Three columns with an entablature and pedestal in a well-head motive.

7 Four columns with an entablature and pedestal in a well-head motive.

8 A well-head with shaft and sculpture in an entrant angle.

9 A well-head in a recess with a shaft and canopy.

10 A well-head with corner columns and a roof, against a wall serving two levels.

11 A well-head within an octagonal columnar edifice.

12 A wall fountain in a niche with basin below.

13 A fountain in a niche with a font and lower basin.

14 A corner niche with water jets emerging from the base of a sculptured figure into a basin below.

15 A wall jet with a lower basin within an order composition.

16 A composition of scrolls, shaft and pediment incorporating a water jet and receiving basin.

17 A wall jet with a lower basin within an order composition.

18 A wall jet within a frame of scrolls and pediment with a lower basin.

19 Wall jets with receiving troughs flanking a doorway.

20 Water jets with receiving basins in a terrace wall serving an upper and lower level, with corner columns and canopy.

21 Wall fountains and receiving tank in a colonnaded gable composition.

22 A wall cascade in a niche and statue composition in an architectural feature.

23 A composition of niches and statues with a series of superimposed water jets with a receiving tank below.

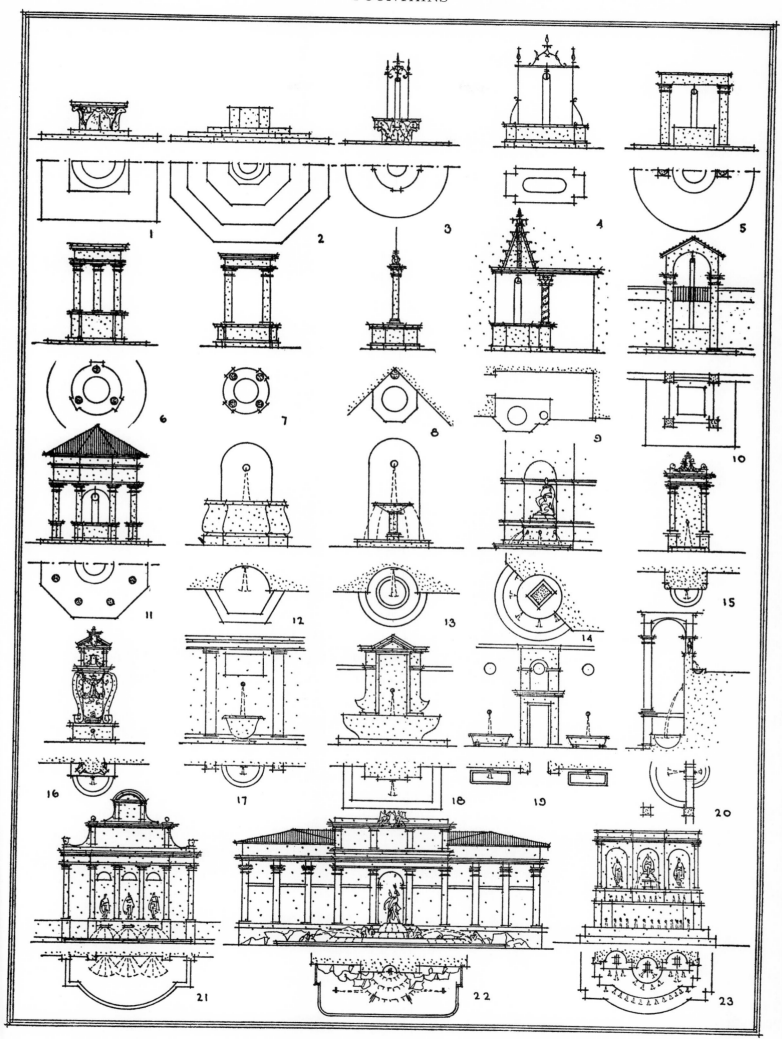

Plate 28

GARDENS

The garden is a piece of ground, open or enclosed, appropriated to the use of plants, flowers or fruits.

Enclosed examples

1 A motive with a central and corner embellishment.

2 The center and enclosure outline emphasized.

3 A pergola or arbor terminating an end with a balanced scheme of borders in front.

4 A concentric circular border scheme at the end of an enclosure.

5 A central panel with corner planting, in combination with a central wall fountain.

6 A semicircular pergola at the end of an enclosure with a fore border motive.

7 A circular end motive, with side planting and a central panel.

8 A semicircular end feature, with corner motives.

9 Side planting with a central panel divided by a circle and paths.

10 Panels, in an end composition about a central pool, in composition with parallel panel compositions.

11 A rectangular composition with side, corner and center emphasis.

12 A composition with the sides more important than the center.

13 An enclosed composition about a circular pool, with borders and paths in balanced features, leading to a higher level.

14 A composition with an end pergola and a pool in a central panel.

15 A circular pool in an end composition, with side, corner and parallel panel planting.

16 An octagonal end composition about a central pool, with side, corner and center panel planting.

17 A large oblong composition with a central panel and octagonal end features, flanked with rows of trees and pergolas at the sides. The ends and corners embellished with connected and balanced motives.

18 A large oblong composition with a central panel, with pools and trees at the ends. Embellished borders, sides and ends, alternate with paths about the central composition.

19 A large oblong composition with semi-circular ends. A central panel with a circular pool at the ends is flanked at the sides with double rows of trees which terminate at the ends in semi-circular pergolas about the pools. The sides, corners and ends are embellished and follow the general contour.

Plate 29

GARDENS

Dealing with border, plat, panel and parterre compositions

1 A square motive divided by diagonals.

2 A circular motive with axes.

3 A rectangular motive with diagonals and axes.

4 A square motive with axes.

5 A central panel with a single border motive.

6 A composition of panels and borders about an open circle and axes.

7 Quadrant border motives.

8 A central panel in an open space, with axial and diagonal open motives.

9 A central feature with balanced panels about the axes.

10 Balanced panels in a square motive.

11 A square motive of balanced panels, within a square with diagonal approach.

12 A circular central panel with diagonal approaches, and axial plat divisions.

13 An oblong motive with borders and central panel.

14 A central feature with a path on axis with plat divisions at right angles.

15 An octagonal panel in combination with circular corner panels.

16 A motive with semicircular ends.

17 A motive combining the square and side circles.

18 A series of borders and paths in a "Labyrinth Motive."

19 A lozenge shaped central panel with side beds.

20 A rectangle and semicircles in an open composition.

21 A rectangular composition of borders or beds.

22 Border motives for semicircular end features.

23 An oblong composition of borders and panels.

24–26 Oblongs with entrant angles in various motives.

25 Central motives in a rectangular composition.

27 Elaborate "Parterre" motives of panels and scrolls.

28 Various shaped panels in a parterre development.

29 A motive with concentric ellipses and axial and diagonal features.

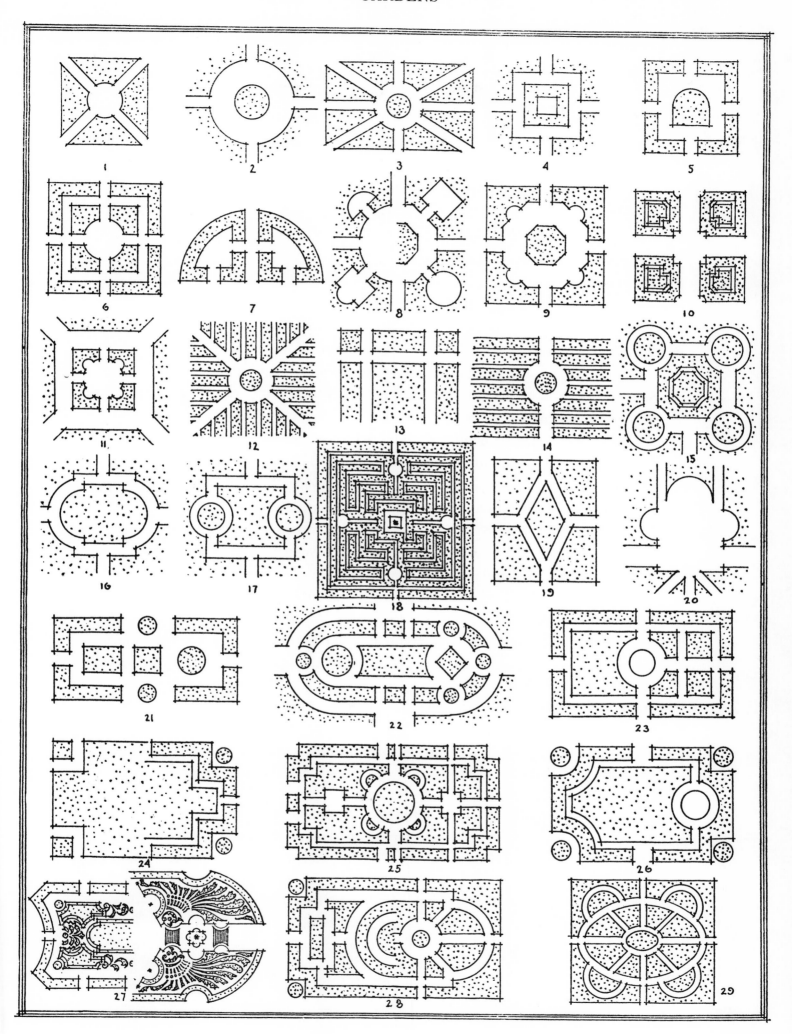

Plate 30

GATEWAYS

The gateway is an entrance in a wall, barrier, fence or the like, such as is intended to be closed by a gate.

1   A huge battlemented wall with a semi-circular opening.

2   A battlemented mass with a large horseshoe arched opening.

3   An elliptical opening in a great wall.

4   A wall with large and small openings.

5   A circular headed opening in a wall with a stepped motive over the opening.

6   A huge fortified tower composition in a wall, with a semi-circular opening.

7   A mass of superimposed stepped and gabled roofs, about and above a wall opening.

8–9   Projecting masses in a wall with arched openings.

10–11   Openings in a wall, flanked with connected circular towers.

12   A salient portal motive, centering a roofed composition with tower ends.

13–15   Towers flanking a connecting portal.

14   A large mass terminating in double towers, with a central opening.

16   A mass with flanking salients, crowned with a domed circular colonnade.

17–18   Openings flanked with piers supporting small towers.

19   An opening in a wall with a domed composition overhead.

20   An opening flanked with columns supporting small towers.

21   An arched opening in a fortified tower projecting beyond a wall.

22   A splay sided arched opening in a wall with an architectural feature above.

23   Coupled orders flanking an archway, with a pediment and dome composition overhead.

24   Coupled orders flanking an opening with an arched attic motive.

25   Orders and scrolls flanking an archway, with a scrolled and pedimented order above.

26   Coupled orders flanking an opening in a stepped composition, crowned with smaller orders and a pediment.

27   An arch within flanking columns and entablature.

28   An arch within flanking columns with an entablature and central sculptural note.

29   Coupled orders flanking an archway, with sculptural emphasis above.

30   Coupled columns flanking an opening, with a pediment and a superimposed pediment motive above.

31   Two openings flanked with orders with a colonnade above with pediment and dome.

32   A large central opening in an order composition, flanked with smaller wall openings.

33   A large and smaller flanking openings, beneath an arcade motive, between projecting pylons.

34   A large and smaller flanking openings between piers with an entablature and attic.

35   Salient wings flanking a mass with an arcaded opening.

36   Superimposed openings flanked with rustication and orders in a pavilion motive.

Plate 31

GATEWAYS

Dealing with the simpler compositions

1   A colonnade flanking an arched mass.

2   A colonnade, with columns grouped at the side of the opening.

3   Coupled orders flanking a metal grille barrier with a central opening.

4   A composition with a central opening and two diminishing side openings, with individual roof treatment.

5   A roof motive upon posts, with a repetition at the sides at a lower level.

6   A mass composition with a central pedimented feature, supported upon columns flanking an arch.

7   Three openings between a series of columns, with statuary and a central pedimented column composition above.

8   Grouped orders supporting sculpture, flanking a metal grille.

9   Four piers supporting statuary, flanking a large central and narrower side spaces.

10   Arches in an order and scroll composition, flanking a grilled space.

11   Columns flanking an open space, with abutting side walls having openings and niches.

12   Connected towers with side gabled buildings, with an arched opening between the towers.

13   Piers flanking an opening in a metal barrier, in turn flanked with tall shafts supporting sculpture.

14   Pedestals at the sides of an opening in a terrance wall, flanked with tall shafts.

15   A high wall with piers supporting vases, at the sides of an opening.

16   Pylons flanking a metal barrier with a central motive.

17   Arched masses supporting sculpture flanking a metal gate.

18   Arched masses with broken pediments, flanking an opening, in a hedge.

19   Rusticated piers, supporting ornament at the sides of a hedge opening.

20   A flight of steps under a domed mass, flanked with smaller, similar motives at the sides.

21   A flight of steps leading to a metal gate between piers in a wall.

22   Piers in a wall flanking an opening.

23   Steps leading to an opening in a wall, with flanking vases.

24   An opening flanked with posts and curved coping ascending to a higher post and wall on either side.

25   An opening in a roofed salient feature in a wall.

26   A wall increasing in height around the head of an opening.

27   An opening in a pedimented salient feature in a wall.

28   A wall increasing in height, and following the outline of a circular headed opening.

29   A recessed arch in a wall, with an increase of height above the opening, supporting a roof.

30   A recessed arch in a wall with scrolls at the sides and a roof above.

31   An arch in a mass with a hipped roof, side walls, increasing in height at the corner returns and ornamented at these corners.

32   A wall in a scroll and pediment composition, with flanking buttresses about an opening.

33   A growing hedge wall with tall trees at the sides of an opening.

34   A hedge wall clipped in an arch motive with flanking ornament.

35   A hedge wall in an arch motive and flanking vertical trees.

36   A metal gate within an arch, in a motive of flanking columns, broken pediment, keystone, scrolls and rustication.

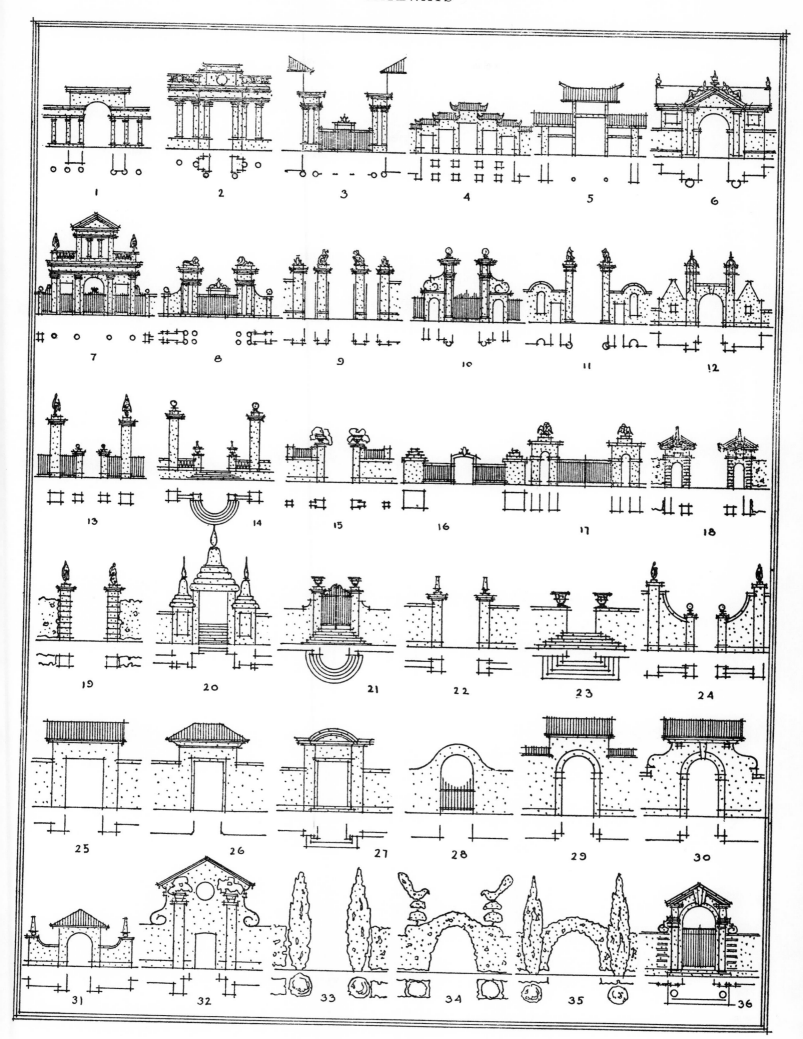

Plate 32

GABLES

The gable is the wall of the building carried up in a triangular termination, to receive the roof when it is not hipped or returned on itself at the ends. When ornamented or made a particular feature it is called a pediment.

Simple gables

1   An end gable with emphasis at the base, following the roof rake.

2–17   An end gable with emphasis at the base and top, following the roof rake.

3   An end gable with a curved outline.

4–5   End gables with curved sides and rounded tops.

6   An end gable with concave sides and rounded top.

7   An end gable following the roof rake, with top emphasis.

8–13   Gables with stepped sides.

9   A combination of side steps and gable.

10   A gable with a pediment termination.

11   An end gable with a pediment and side scroll motive.

12   An end gable with sloping sides and semi-circular termination.

14   An end gable with various curves at the sides.

15   A stepped gable with the copings emphasized.

16   A stepped gable with emphasized copings and corner and central turrets.

18   A gable with emphasis at the base, apex, and along the central wall.

19   An end gable with coupled chimneys at the apex.

20   An end gable with emphasis at the base and on the side rake.

21   An end gable with a cornice following the rake.

22   An end gable with a barge board and half timber.

23   A gable with unequal slopes.

24   A truncated gable end.

25   An end gable following the outline of a gambrel roof with projecting eaves.

26   A gambrel roof gable end, with concave sides.

27   A gambrel roof dormer gable.

28   A side gable springing at the roof eaves.

29   An end gable with an apron.

30   An end gable in combination with a lean to.

31   A gable with projecting stories supported upon brackets.

32   A truncated gable with projecting stories.

33–36   End gables with side chimney motives.

34   An end gable with a corner tower and balanced side chimneys.

35   End gable with a central chimney group and side steps.

37–38   Dormer motives.

39   Dormers in combination with a gable end, but divided by the roof eaves.

Plate 33

GABLES

Dealing with grouped and combined gables

1 An octagonal bay with each face gabled.

2 An end gable with unequal legs.

3 A gable projecting beyond the wall face, supported upon brackets.

4 A gable with an apron, a bay upon brackets and an overhead projection.

5 A gable with a double projection above a bay window.

6 A gable with side eaves above a bay window, in combination with a smaller gable at the side supported upon brackets.

7 A gable in a composition with a gabled bay window at the side.

8 A gable with projecting stories in composition with a corner tower.

9 A gable with a corner turret and chimney.

10 A gable, bay window and corner tower composition.

11 A gable and bay window with projecting stories in a dissymmetric composition.

12 A gable in combination with a gabled side motive.

13–16 A gable in composition with a side salient, with a hipped roof.

14 Two gables of unequal height in combination.

15 A composition of a large central gable, with flanking side gables.

17 A salient with a roof return, in combination with a flat roof gable.

18 Projecting twin gables above twin dormers.

19 A side and end gable in combination.

20 Triple gables of equal height in combination.

21 A composition of three gables, all unequal in mass.

22 Three gables in combination, the central one projecting but smaller.

23 Twin gables between chimneys and with a hood at the center.

24 Twin gables in combination with a third central projecting gable.

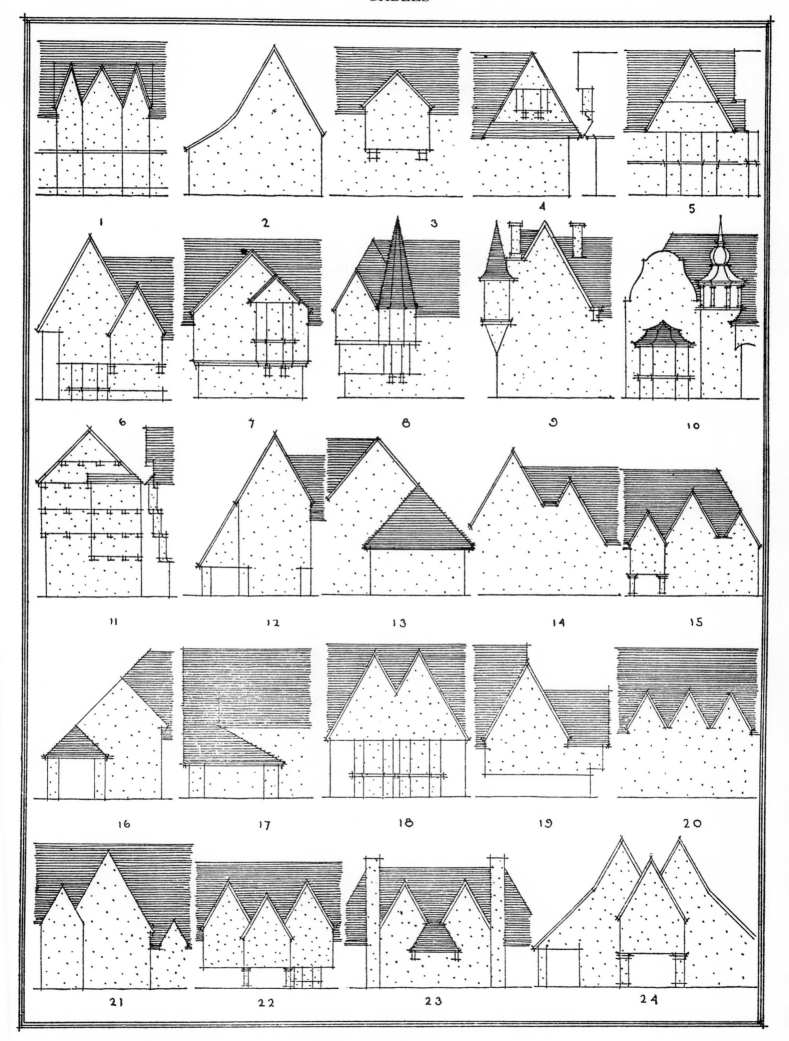

1

2

3

4

5

6

7

8

9

10

11

12

13

14

15

16

17

18

19

20

21

22

23

24

Plate 34

HOODS

The hood is a projection of a sort, above an opening, serving as a protection against the weather.

1   A moulding above a doorway, serving as a shallow hood.

2–3   Bracketed projecting plinths as hoods.

4   A semicircular voussoired hood supported upon brackets.

5   A balcony above a doorway serving as a hood.

6–7   Projecting horizontal roof members above doorways, serving as hoods.

8   The roof slope prolonged over the doorway in a hood motive.

9   A roof with a single slope above a doorway, supported upon side brackets.

10   A hood with hips above a doorway, supported upon side brackets.

11   A truncated hood with compound side slopes.

12   An octagonal pyramidal hood supported upon brackets.

13   A hood with concave sides, supported upon brackets.

14   A hood gabled at three sides and with groined vaulting underneath.

15   An octagonal gabled hood with an ornamented spire.

16   A screen hood above a wall niche.

17   A hipped roof supported upon columns, with a conical end.

18   A pediment incorporated in a horizontal roof band serving as a hood.

19   A pediment supported upon brackets serving as a hood.

20   A projecting gable above a doorway in a hood motive.

21   A barrel vaulted motive penetrating a horizontal roof band, supported upon trellis.

22   A semi-circular pediment supported upon columns serving as a hood.

23   A barrel hood above a doorway, incorporated in a wall overhang.

24   A flat sloping surface, hung with rods above a doorway, serving as a canopy.

25   A flat semi-circular sloping surface, hung with rods above a doorway, serving as a canopy or hood.

Plate 35

PARAPETS

The parapet is a low solid wall, erected at the edge of raised platforms, terraces, bridges, stairs, etc., and above cornices, as a protection against falling. Where it is used as an architectural feature it becomes more or less decorated, and incorporated in the composition.

1   A plain wall with a coping.

2   Panels, carving and inscriptions in a plain wall.

3   A crenellated termination.

4   Solid panels with open spaces between.

5   A crenellated parapet supported upon corbels and arches.

6   A plain wall pierced in a design limited by the material.

7–8   Parapets used as a cornice, in carved and pierced designs.

9   A solid wall with pedestals and panels.

10   Pedestals and open panels, horizontal and inclined.

11   An open parapet of dwarf columns.

12   An inclined example with columns resting upon treads.

13   An inclined example with balusters resting upon brackets.

14   An incline with stepped parapet.

15   Grouped balusters in alternation.

16   Inclined cheek with open panels.

17   Grouped pedestals and balusters.

18   Alternating pedestals and panels, with emphasis on the pedestals.

19   Alternating pedestals and balusters, with pedestals emphasized.

20   A solid wall interrupted with large masses.

21   A balustrade with a fountain and statuary terminal motive.

22   A transition from a lower to a higher solid wall.

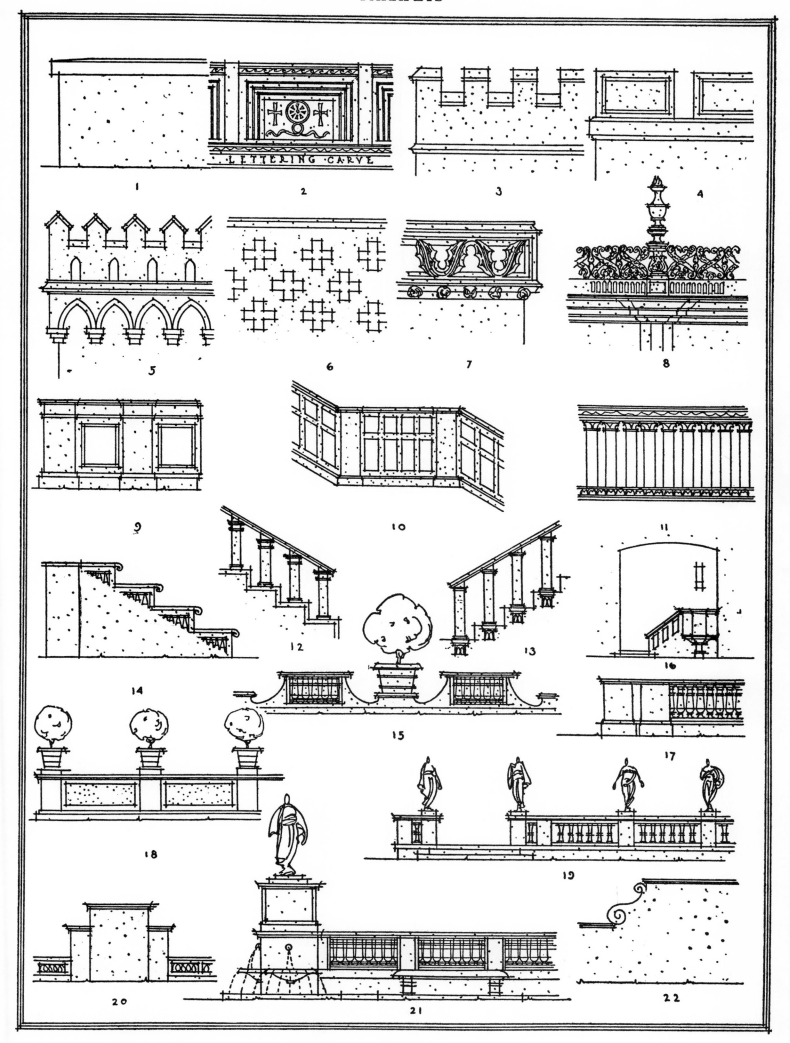

LETTERING CARVE

Plate 36

PAVILIONS

The tent or marquee was the oldest pavilion, then came the shelter, kiosk or summer house and finally the elaborate domed or pedimented edifices incorporated in a building facade.

1   A wall seat with an overhead covering.

2–6   A seat enclosed on three sides with a roof.

3   A free standing octagonal semi-enclosed shelter.

4   An enclosed octagonal building.

5   A roofed circular colonnade.

7   A semi-enclosed shelter upon a bridge.

8   An enclosed oblong building with central emphasis.

9   Shelters with dominant roofs flanking a pergola.

10   A semi-enclosed shelter at the entrant angle of a wall.

11   A free standing edifice with gables and cupola.

12   Shelters flanking an entrance.

13–14   Shelters along an enclosing wall.

15   A shelter terminating a flight of steps.

16   An octagonal building having two stories.

Plate 37

PAVILIONS

Dealing with the domed or pedimented edifices incorporated in a building facade

1 A motive with the entrance and roof emphasized.

2 The second story made dominant.

3 A colonnade with a central archway.

4 A pediment and pedestal combined with a colonnade.

5 Projecting surface and superimposed orders.

6 A portico used as a note.

7 An octagonal motive.

8 Superimposed orders with a gable or pediment.

9 Coupled orders emphasizing the second story and a pedimented attic.

10 A motive with the orders and sculpture terminated with a pediment.

11 A pediment only emphasizing the composition.

12 Corner tourelles used in combination with a roof mass.

13 A pavilion with the corners treated with superimposed orders, gables, dormers and cupolas.

14 The second floor made important by columns and statuary and further emphasized by a cupola upon a dome and drum.

15 Superimposed orders and a dormer in an unusual composition.

16 A composition in which the first floor, corners and roof is embellished.

17 A pedimented colonnade above an entrance.

18 Superimposed coupled orders with statuary and a decorated pediment.

19 An importance placed upon the first and last stories.

20 Orders extending through several stories for emphasis.

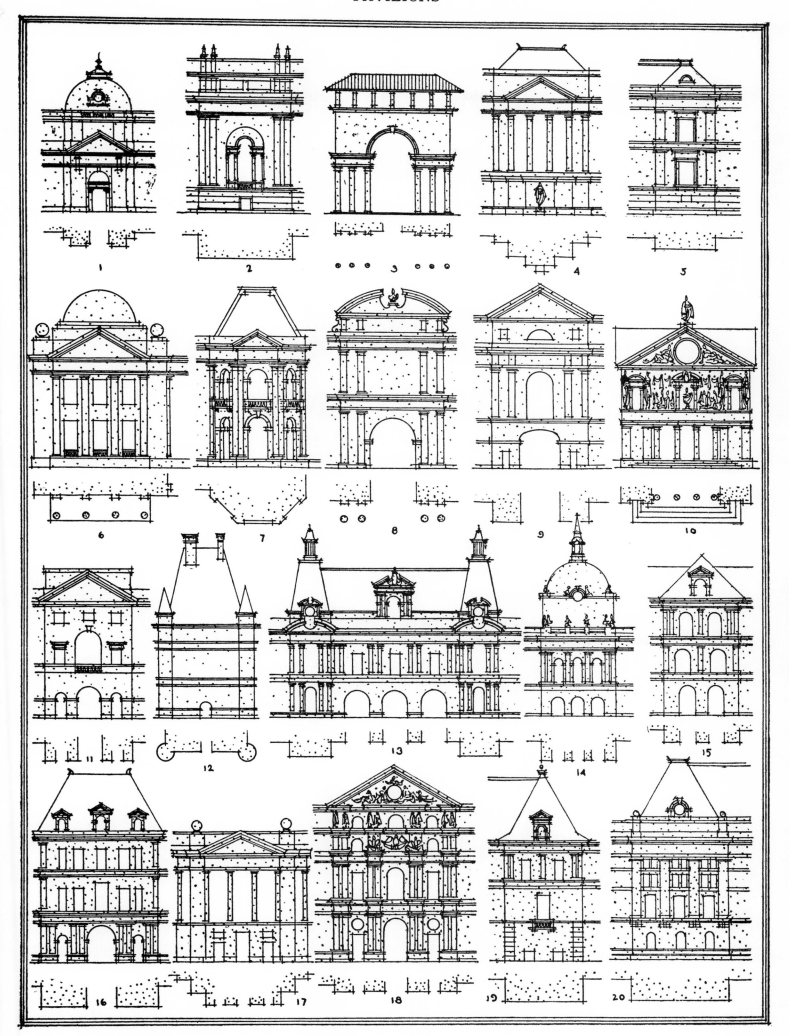

Plate 38

PEDESTALS

The pedestal is used as a support for an object, and its composition depends on the relation and importance to that object. Natural settings, such as a boulder or cliff are to be considered as well as architectural ones.

1–3–4–5–22   Shaft motives used as pedestals.

2–10   Concentric superimposed pedestals, in a fountain motive.

6–9   An oblong mass with base and cap and side emphasis.

7–11   A low circular base with a superimposed composition.

8   Circular steps with diagonal emphasis and a central shaft.

12   A pedestal with corner orders.

13   A pedestal with sculptured figures as side supports.

14   A pedestal with an end baluster motive.

15   A pedestal composed of a core with diagonal corner orders.

16   A square mass with pedimented entrance motives on the sides.

17   Superimposed pedestals with a fountain motive at the termination of a balustrade.

18   A mass with cap and base at an angle in a balustrade.

19   A mass at the intersection of a parapet and a flight of steps, serving as a pedestal.

20–21   Entrance doorways in a wall mass serving as pedestals.

23   A semi-circular parapet supported upon an arch, with supporting figures at the sides.

24   A niche in a wall with an oblong mass therein, serving as a pedestal.

25   A mass supported upon a corbel, with flanking motives.

26   A plinth supported upon brackets in a wall embrasure, serving as a pedestal.

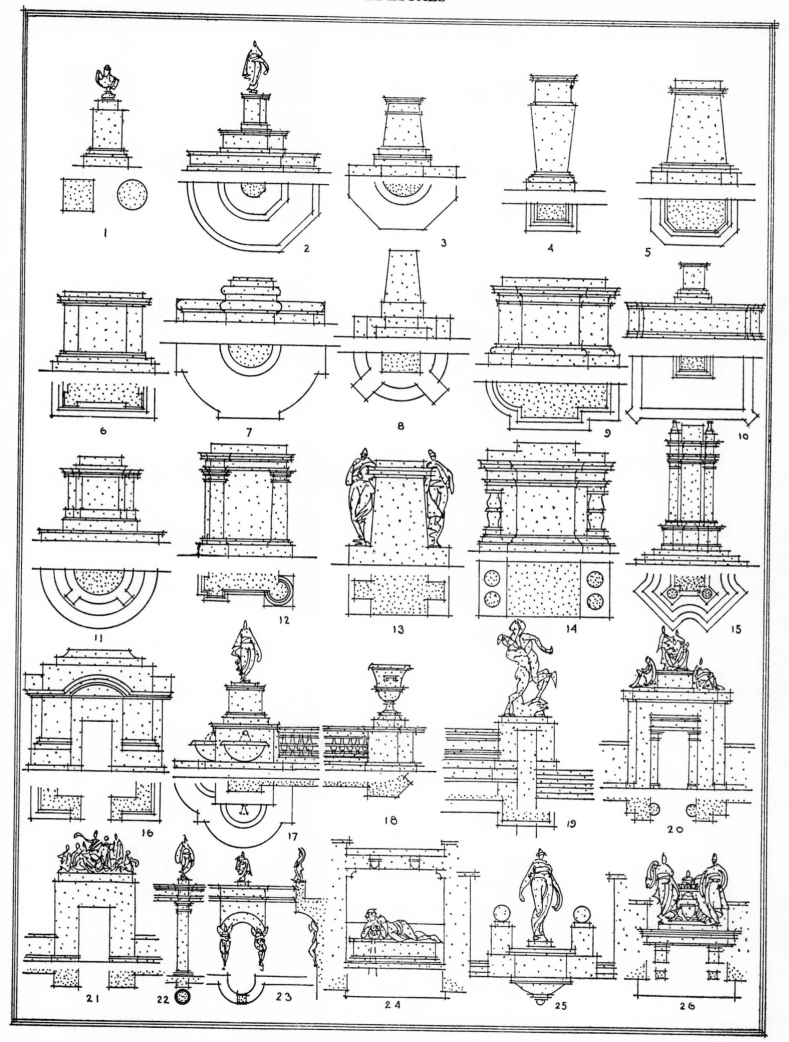

Plate 39

PLANS

The plan is a horizontal indication of the relative position of the walls and partitions of a building or group of buildings.

Dealing with salients

1   A square mass with slight central salients.

2   A square mass with slightly projecting corners.

3   A circular mass with axial emphasis.

4   An octagonal mass with axial emphasis.

5–6   A square mass with axial emphasis, by means of semi-circular wings.

7   A square and semi-circular mass in combination.

8–9–10   Cruciform masses with various methods of emphasis.

11   An oblong mass with elaborated sides and end wings.

12   A square mass with elaborated sides and corners.

13   A rectangular mass with central salients.

14   A "T" shaped mass.

15   An oblong mass with frontal end salients.

16   An "U" shaped mass.

17   An "H" shaped mass.

18   An "U" shaped mass with a central rear wing.

19   An "L" shaped mass.

20   A "T" shaped mass with unequal arms and a corner diagonal wing.

21   A square mass with axial wings.

22   An oblong mass with various end salients.

23   A "Z" shaped mass.

24   An oblong mass with slight frontal salients at the ends and rear end diagonal wings.

25   A mass with parallel end and central wings.

26   An oblong mass with diagonal end wings and central salients.

27   An "H" shaped mass with end salients.

28   An "H" shaped mass with central emphasis at the rear.

29   A central mass with "T" shaped lateral wings.

30   A central mass with side and rear "T" shaped wings.

31   An "U" shaped composition with a central mass.

32   A central mass with parallel side wings at right angles to the mass.

33   An "H" shaped mass with end wings and a central wing at the rear, combining with a series of parallel wings.

34   A composition in which the "H" and "T" type plans are combined.

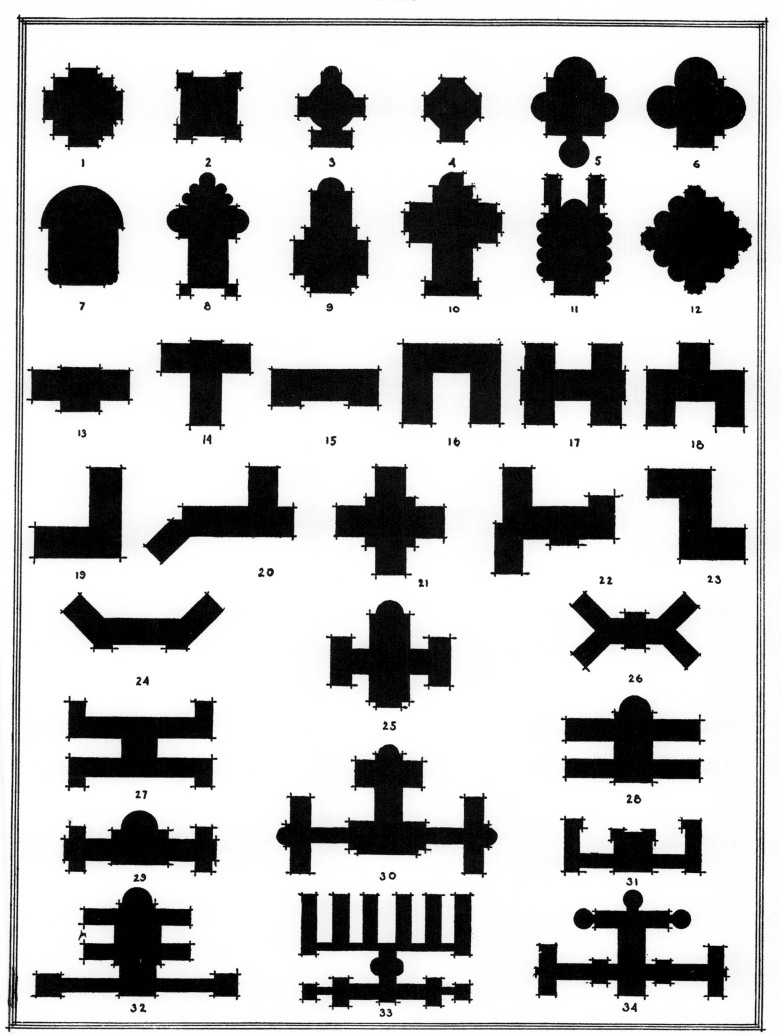

Plate 40

PLANS

Dealing with compositions having fore courts

1   A "V" shaped mass with a walled fore court in the entrant angle.

2   A "L" shaped mass with a walled fore court in the entrant angle.

3   An "H" shaped mass with outstanding buildings at the ends of the wings, producing a fore court.

4–9   An "U" shaped composition with a fore court between the wings.

5   A semi-circular court with fore and central mass compositions.

6   A central mass in combination with front and rear "U" types, producing a fore and a rear court.

7   "U" and "T" types in a composition, producing a fore and outer side courts.

8   A central mass with corner masses in combination with "L" type frontal corner salients, producing a fore court and side courts.

10   A central mass with flanking compositions forming a double fore court.

11–13   A fore court between elaborated wings of an "U" type mass with a central composition.

12   Balanced compositions about three sides of a rectangular fore court.

14   A fore court between the wings of a balanced composition, with an independent mass in the center of the open side of the court.

15   A group composition of "U" shaped masses around a fore court partly enclosed by two independent masses on the open side of the court.

16   A group of three "U" shaped masses about an independent central mass.

17   A central mass with corner "L" type extensions enclosing a court which is partly enclosed by independent masses on the free side.

18   A central mass with lateral extensions in combination with a series of wings in a "fret motive," producing three fore courts.

19   An oblong fore court with balanced compositions at the sides.

20   Three "U" shaped masses in a composition producing a central fore court and similar minor ones at the sides.

21   A balanced composition with a fore court with semi-circular sides and a central mass.

22   A fore court leading to a central court in a balanced composition.

23   A composition of connected groups about a court open at the center of a side opposite the dominant feature.

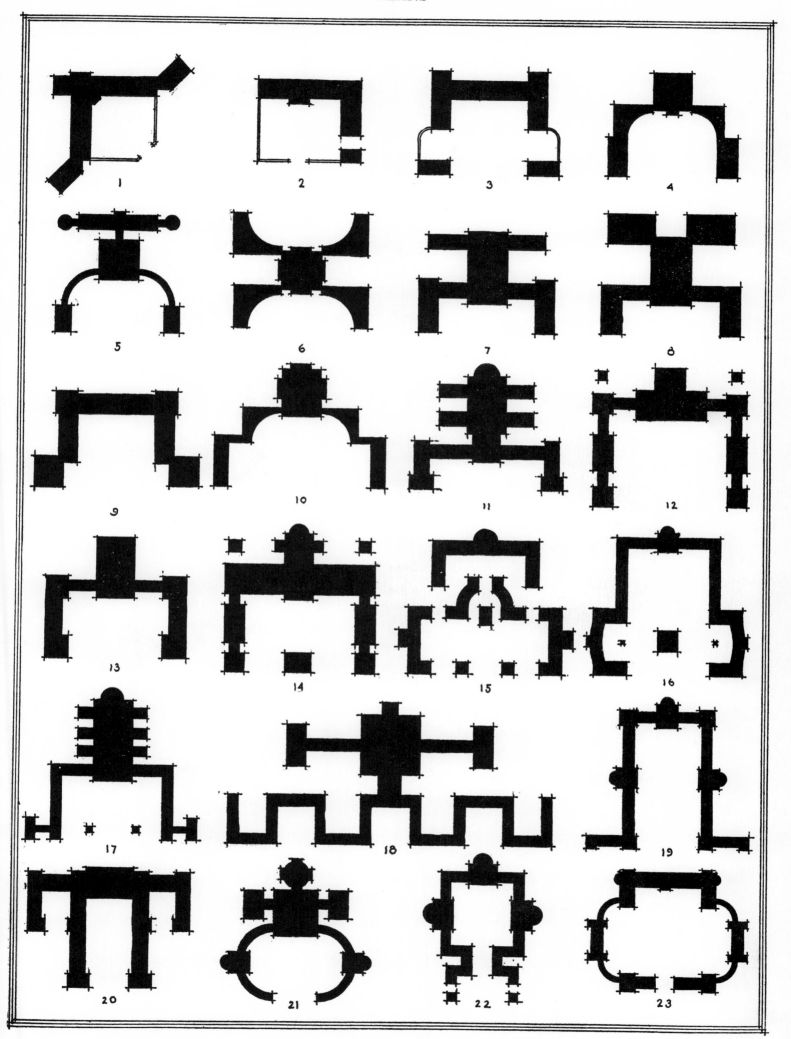

Plate 41

PLANS

Dealing with compositions having interior courts

1 An annular mass with axial salients.

2 A pentagonal mass with a circular court and corner salients.

3–4 Hollow square masses with corner salients.

5 An "U" shaped composition with corner emphasis, enclosed by a wall on the fourth side against which a corner-emphasized mass rests.

6 A cruciform and hollow square mass in composition, with interior courts.

7 "T" and "U" types in composition with interior courts at the sides.

8 An "H" shaped mass in composition with front and rear wings parallel to the cross bar of the "H," having two interior courts.

9 Front and rear central compositions, in combination with an oblong mass grouped about an interior court.

10 An "U" type mass with similar masses at the sides, forming two interior courts at the sides.

11–12 Wings grouped about an oblong court, divided by a central mass.

13 An "U" shaped mass with a similar composition at the rear, divided by a central mass.

14 An oblong group about three interior courts, with a rear composition.

15 An oblong group massed about five interior courts.

16 An oblong group around a court in composition with "U" and "T" types forming a mass with eight interior courts.

17 Three rectangular groups in combination with dividing parallel wings, making a group with ten interior courts.

18 Concentric rectangular groups in a composition with four interior courts.

19 A rectangular court group combined with similar divided groups at the sides, and with rear emphasis by wings and a central mass.

20 A composition of "H," "T" and "U" masses about central courts.

21 Divided rectangular masses about courts flanking a similar undivided mass in composition with a rear group about a square court with semi-circular side wings.

22 Divided rectangular masses about courts flanking a similar undivided mass in composition with a cruciform mass at the rear.

23 A group around a rectangular court, divided by a cruciform mass, with divided "U" type masses at the ends.

24 A mass grouped about a rectangle divided by a cruciform mass with a projecting rear composition.

25–26 Divided "U" type compositions, on three sides of an enclosed square.

27 A divided rectangular group in composition with a square group with side wings.

28 A central mass with an interior court with divided "U" type groups at the sides.

29 A group around a square with semi-circular side wings on three sides, with an "U" shaped group on the remaining side, and diagonal side wings.

30 A rectangular composition with "T" shaped end masses, and front and rear divided "U" type groups.

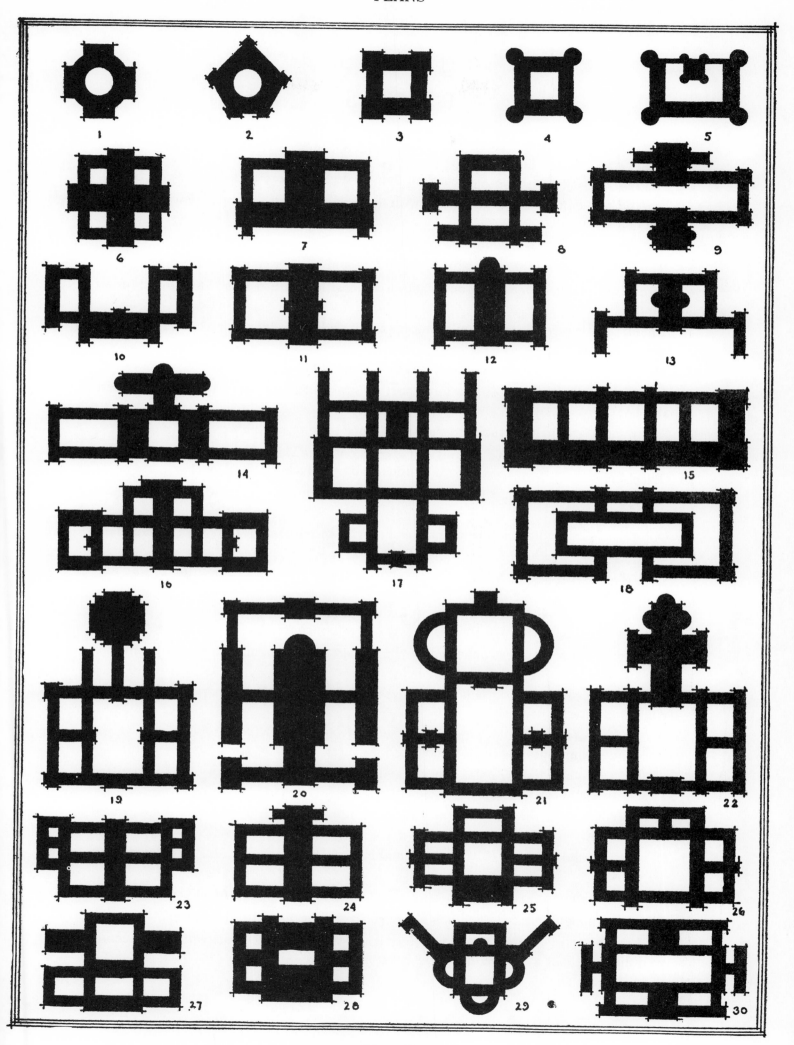

Plate 42

PLANS

Dealing with groups having fore and interior courts

1   "U" and "T" shaped masses in combination producing a fore and side interior courts.

2   Two "U" type masses in combination with a central mass, in a composition with a fore court and side interior courts.

3–4   "H" and "T" types in compositions with a fore and side interior courts.

5   "U" shaped masses in a composition with a fore and interior courts at the sides.

6   Three hollow square masses in a balanced composition with a fore court and interior courts.

7   A main "U" type mass with similar masses on the sides, producing three interior courts and a fore court.

8   An "U" type mass with side masses grouped about two inner courts.

9   Semi-circular masses enclosing a fore court with a central oblong composition divided axially producing interior courts.

10   Rectangular groups with inner courts about three sides of a square.

11   A square central court with rectangular groups on three sides divided into two interior courts, with salients on the free side of the square producing a fore court.

12   Free standing, oblong, and fret shaped masses in a composition with fore and interior courts.

13   Oblong, square and semi-circular masses, in a balanced composition with a dominant central mass, in a fore and interior court motive.

14   Oblong concentric masses with central connecting masses, in a composition of fore and interior courts.

15   A hollow "U" type mass with central features and interior courts, grouped about an interior court, with side salient masses forming a fore court.

16   A central dominant mass connected at the corners to rectangular groups with interior courts.

17   Independent and balanced hollow square masses in a grouped composition with a fore court and interior courts.

18   A central feature enclosed with parallel wings connecting to "U" type masses at the sides, in a composition with fore and interior courts.

19   An "U" type and hollow oblong mass connected by a central feature in a composition having fore and interior courts.

20   A fore court with receding side masses in combination with a "T" and oblong mass composition.

21–22–24   "T" and hollow "U" types in combination in an interior and fore court composition

23   Hollow rectangular masses grouped about a fore court having a central end feature.

25   Hollow rectangular masses flanking a fore court with a central end feature.

26–27   Interior court motives flanking a fore court with a central end feature connecting to a motive about a rectangular inner court.

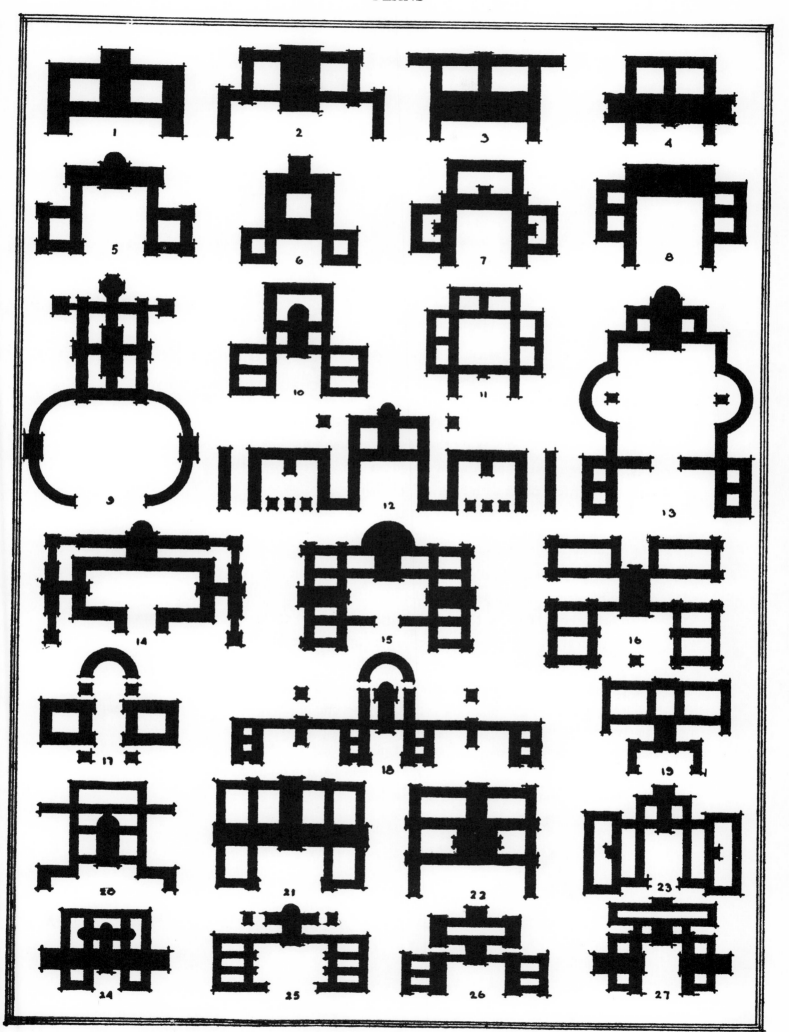

Plate 43

PLAZAS

The plaza is an open square or market place having one or more levels; approached in various ways by avenues, streets, inclines or stairs, singly or in combination.

1 A symmetrical plaza between lateral approaches.

2 A symmetrical plaza with axial approaches.

3 A symmetrical plaza with an axial approach and another at right angles at one end.

4 A circular plaza with diagonal approaches.

5 A circular plaza with radial approaches of varying importance.

6 A circular plaza with axial, diagonal and an end lateral approach.

7 A dissymmetrical plaza with corner approaches.

8 A symmetrical plaza with approaches at the corners.

9 An oblong plaza with a semi-circular end and end diagonal approaches giving balance to a dissymmetrical scheme.

10 An oblong plaza with parallel lateral approaches and an end axial one.

11 A dissymmetrical scheme with an attempt at balance.

12 An unbalanced scheme, but with a feature giving more or less a sense of balance.

13 A symmetrical plaza with balanced diagonal approaches at the ends.

14 An irregular oblong plaza, with a secondary balanced scheme therein.

15 A symmetrical triangular plaza with corner diagonal approaches.

16 An oblong plaza in combination with a smaller one of irregular outline, with balanced approaches to the larger.

17 Intersecting approaches forming a small plaza.

18 A balanced scheme with end diagonal approaches and end lateral approaches.

19 An elliptical plaza with balanced approaches.

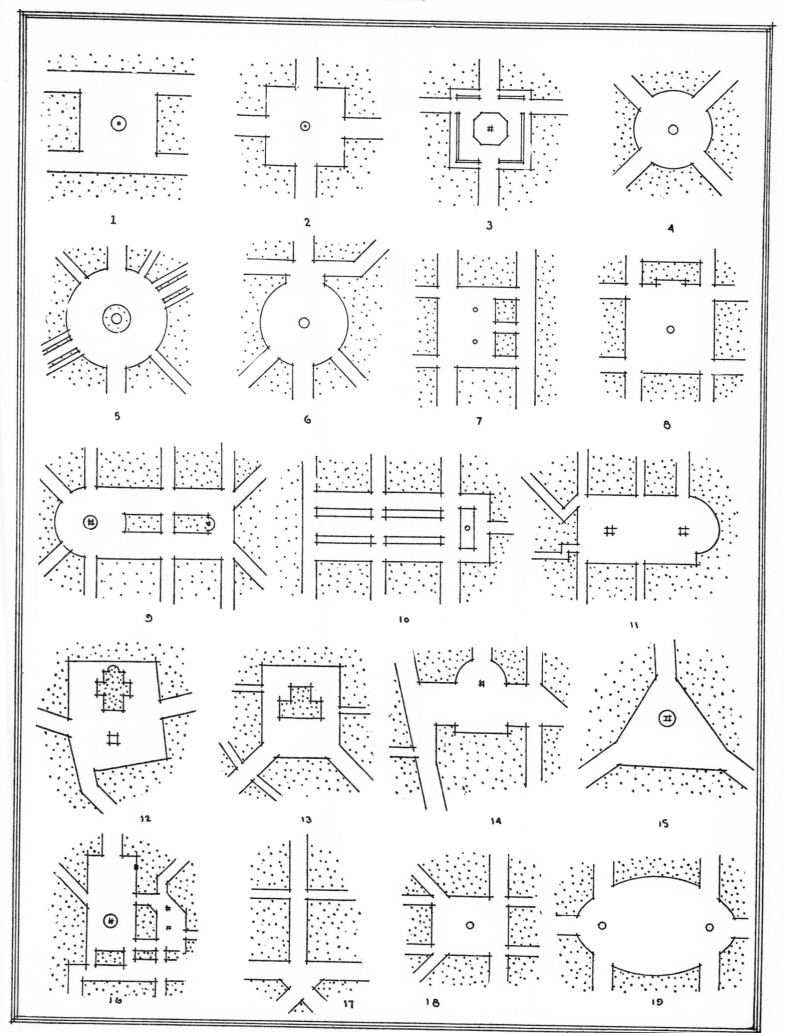

Plate 44

PLAZAS

Dealing with groups and different levels

1 A plaza of irregular outline, about an edifice, with the main approaches terminating with this edifice.

2 A balanced lateral and oblong plaza in combination.

3 A balance scheme with diagonal end approaches and an axial one.

4 A plaza with semi-circular ends, with balanced approaches.

5 An enclosed plaza with an approach from one end.

6 An edifice in an irregularly shaped open space, balanced by a lesser motive on axis.

7 A balanced semi-circular plaza, with secondary streets following the outline.

8 A balanced plaza with dissimilar lateral and end approaches.

9 A balanced plaza with approaches from three sides, with a feature terminating the approaches.

10 Three plazas in a composition forming a balanced whole.

11 A balanced plaza with stairway approaches.

12 Upper and lower plazas with lateral stairway approaches.

13 A plaza with a direct stairway approach and with lateral ramps.

14 Upper and lower plazas between an ascending roadway.

15 A balanced plaza at the summit of an ascending roadway and a monumental flight of steps and ramps.

16 A plaza between salients of a building and a bridge head, with lateral communication to a lower level.

17 A flight of steps and side ramps leading to a semi-circular plaza at a higher level.

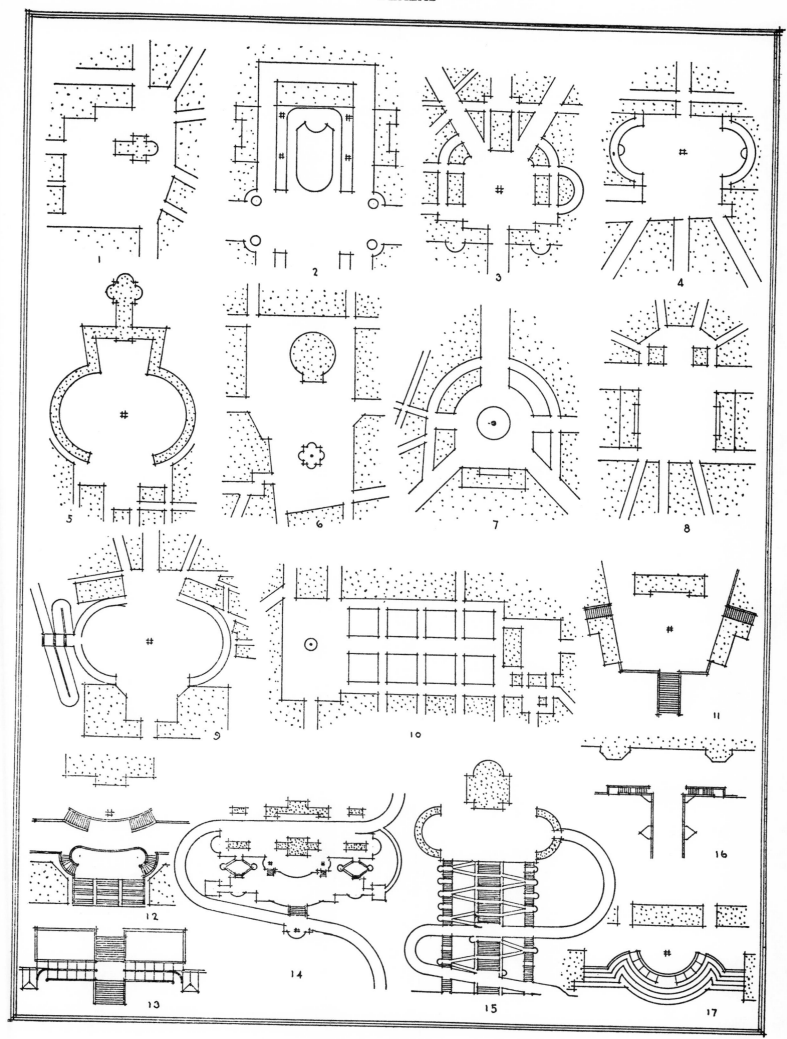

Plate 45

PORCHES

The porch is a roofed entrance, either incorporated in a building or applied as a feature to a building.

Dealing with incorporated examples

1 A barrel vault in the side of an edifice serving as a porch.

2 A barrel vault with side columns in the side of an edifice.

3 A hexagonal motive, with a canopy, half of which is recessed in the building.

4 An arcade serving as a porch.

5–18 A loggia motive.

6–7 Colonnade motives.

8–9–10 Recessed motives with columns and entablatures.

11 A roofed recess in an entrant angle.

12–16 A porch incorporated in the side of a gable.

13 The first story of a wing serving as a porch.

14 A salient with a gambrel roof supported upon columns.

15 A salient with a ridge roof supported upon columns.

17 An exterior stair landing used as a porch, roofed with a projection of the main roof.

19 A combination of stair and loggia motives.

20 The end of a ridge roof prolonged as a covering for a porch.

21–27 A second story loggia motive.

22 A superimposed loggia motive.

23 A two-storied circular porch with columns and an entablature.

24 An arcade motive with central emphasis.

25 An arcade in combination with a corner arcade above.

26 An upper and lower porch in a projecting feature.

28 An upper porch incorporated in the slope of a roof.

29 A porch incorporated in a roof gable.

30 A porch incorporated in a gable above a bay.

Plate 46

PORCHES

Dealing with examples applied to the building

1   A half-timbered salient with a roof with one slope.

2   A motive with free standing columns under a pediment.

3   A colonnade with its individual roof.

4   A roofed salient with access at the sides.

5   A motive with columns, entablature, balustrade and corner piers.

6   Examples of columns with an entablature and attic.

7   An octagonal motive with columns and pointed roof.

8   A circular motive with columns and entablature.

9   A colonnade with a circular central feature.

10 An octagonal end feature with columns and a hipped roof.

11–15 Gabled motives.

12 A loggia motive with central emphasis.

13 A pedimented portico having two stories.

14 An arcade motive.

16 A loggia above a salient.

17 Lateral stairways and landing incorporated in a porch composition.

18 A pedimented portico above a salient feature.

19 A colonnade with central emphasis and a smaller superimposed colonnade. ·

20 An upper porch around a salient feature, supported upon corbels.

21 A roof with a gable outline upon columns.

22 A gable motive with lateral buttresses.

23 A loggia motive with a central tower.

24 A buttressed loggia motive.

25 A loggia at the head of lateral stairways, with a superimposed loggia motive.

26 A three-storied arch motive with a gable termination.

27 A triangular motive with a canopy.

28 An octagonal arcaded porch with a dome and cupola.

Plate 47

ROOFS

The roof is that part of the closure of a building which covers it from the sky.

Dealing with various types employed

1–32   A lean-to roof.

2   A ridged roof.

3   A ridged roof with a lower lean-to roof.

4   A ridged roof with unequal slopes.

5   A low hipped roof, with the hips meeting at the center.

6   A roof with concave hips and a cupola.

7–8   Roofs with a ridge and end hips.

9   No. 8 elaborated with a dormer and cupola.

10–21   A hipped roof with a deck.

11   A roof with hips and valleys.

12   A roof with an ornamented ridge and convex hips.

13   A hipped roof with a double slope.

14   A hipped roof with composite slopes.

15–16   A combination of gabled and hip roof.

17   A jerkinhead roof.

18   A ridge or gabled roof with a prolongation of a slope in a lean-to motive.

19   A gambrel roof.

20   A barrel roof.

22   A hipped roof with hips having a double curve.

23   A pavilion roof with a lantern.

24   An octagonal hipped roof.

25   An octagonal hipped roof with a lantern.

26   Superimposed octagonal roofs with concave hips.

27   A hipped spire with two slopes and chamfered corners.

28   Superimposed roofs with concave eaves and hips.

29   A conical roof.

30   A domical roof with stepped base.

31   A bulbous roof with ascending spiral ribs.

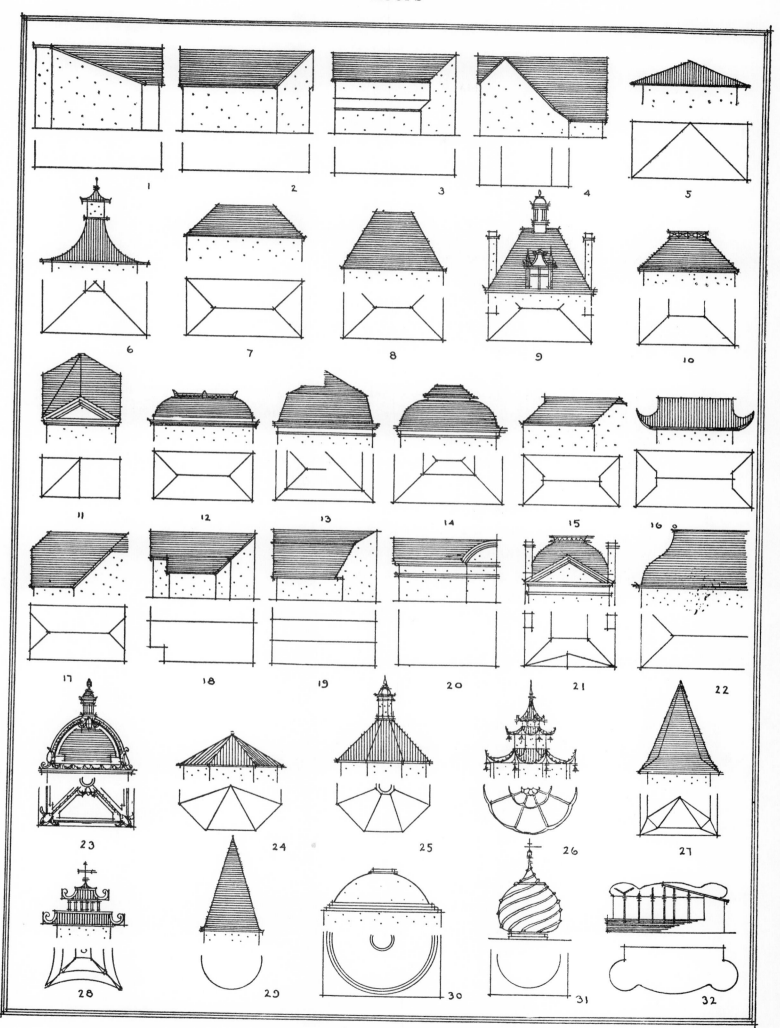

Plate 48

ROOFS

Dealing with compositions above wall surfaces with the wall in the same plane

1   A ridge or gable roof.
2   A ridge roof with end hips.
3   A ridge roof with a gable end and a hipped end.
4   A gable roof with unequal ridges.
5   A roof with unequal ridges and hipped and gable ends.
6   A roof with a hipped end and a gable end with a lean-to continuation.
7   A roof with hipped ends of unequal slope.
8   A gable roof with a lean-to continuation at one end.
9   A roof with unequal ridges and a hipped end and a gable end with a lean-to continuation.
10   A hipped roof with a lean-to end projection and a gable in the slope of the other end.
11   A hipped roof with unequal ends.
12   A ridge roof with a jerkin head end and a gable and hipped end.
13   A gable end and a gable and hipped end in a ridge roof.
14   A hipped roof with eaves at different levels.
15   A gable roof with hips at one end and a lean-to and gable roof motive at the other.
16   A gable roof with lean-to motives at the ends.
17   A hipped roof with lean-to motives at the ends.
18   A hipped roof in combination with a lower gable roof.
19   A gable roof in combination with a similar lower roof with hipped-end and a lean-to extension.
20   Gabled roofs of different height with a lean-to end.
21   A hipped roof with a gable end in combination with a similar one at a lower level with a lean-to projection.
22   Gable roofs of decreasing heights in a composition.
23   A gable roof with lower hipped roofs at the ends.
24   A hipped roof with a gable roof continuation and a small hip at the end.
25   A gable, a gable roof and a lower hipped roof in combination.
26   Twin gables or an "M" roof in the side of a ridge.
27   "M" roofs in the side of a ridge roof.
28   A hipped roof with eaves at different levels and corner gables.
29   A gable roof with side gables.
30   A hipped roof with end gables and lean-tos.
31   A gable roof with similar lower ones at the ends with small hips in a gable motive.

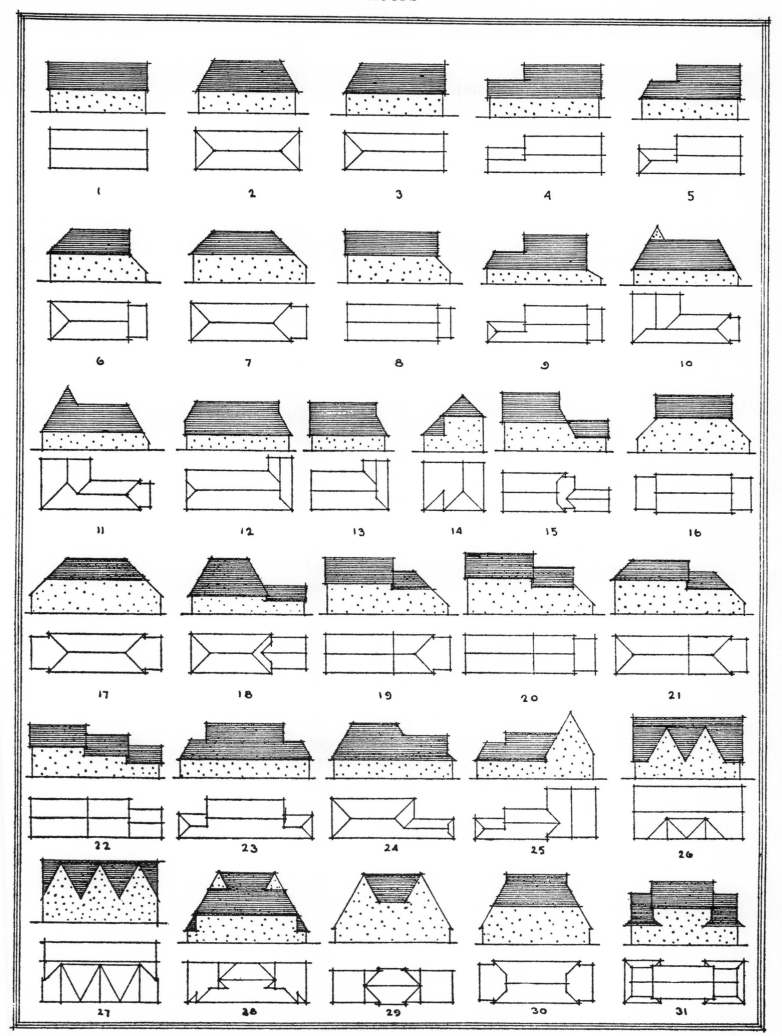

Plate 49

ROOFS

Dealing with compositions having wings and salients

1. Gable roofs at right angles, with one higher than the other.
2. Hipped roofs at right angles, with one roof higher than the other.
3. A gable roof with a lower hipped roof with lean-to.
4. An "U" shaped composition with hipped ends and a gable roofed central mass.
5. An "H" shaped composition with gabled roofs and a central lean-to feature.
6. A "Z" shaped composition with gable roofs.
7. A hollow square composition with gable roofs.
8. A hipped roof with a gable end intersected by a similar one with a lower ridge.
9. An "H" and hollow square group with gable roofs.
10. A gable roof with a hipped roof wing.
11. A hipped roof with gable roofed wings.
12. An "H" shaped composition with hipped roof and upper end gables.
13. A gable roof with a projecting slope over a salient central mass.
14. An "H" shaped composition with gable roofs, the central mass with unequal slopes.
15. A mass with end salients with a hipped roof.
16. A mass with end wings with a jerkin head roof.
17. A mass with hipped roof and lean-to motives at the center and ends.
18. A mass with end salients with a jerkin head roof, and lean-to roof over a high central mass.
19. A composition with diagonal end wings, with a gable roof and also a hipped roof.
20. An "U" shaped mass with lateral end wings with hipped roofs.
21. An "U" shaped mass with corner wings and hipped roofs.
22. A central mass with lateral wings with gambrel roofs.
23. An "M" roof in the side of a gambrel roof with lean-to roofs over the dormers.
24. A central salient with flanking gables with gable roofs.

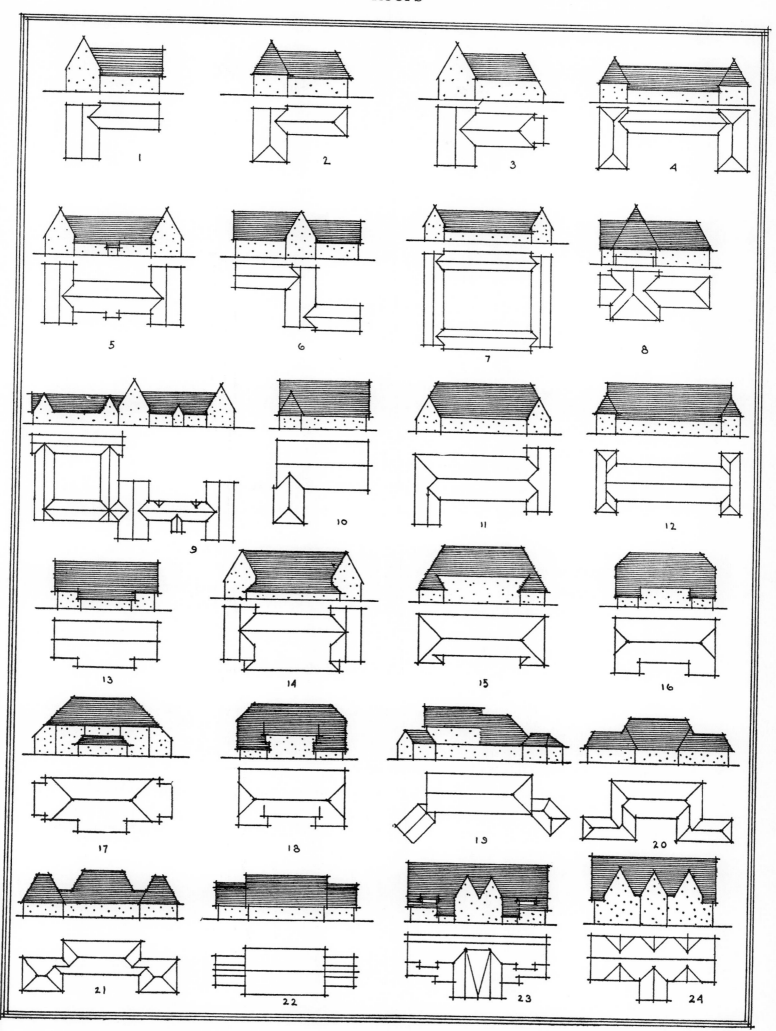

Plate 50

SEATING

Seating is the disposal or placing of large or small numbers of people on benches or chairs, within an open, enclosed or semi-enclosed space with proper regard to the visual and aural conditions imposed by the purpose of such an assembly.

1   A small group within a rectangle, side aisles, light and entrances and a level floor.

2   A small group within a rectangle, side and central aisles, light from two sides, end entrance and level floor.

3   A group with two side and two inner aisles, with light on three sides and an entrance on the remaining side, level or inclined floor. Seats curved for better visual lines.

4   Central and side aisles, serving a group with light from two sides and access at the corners. Level floor.

5   A group within a square with central aisle and aisles on three sides with corridors on all sides. Level, inclined, or curved floors.

6   A grouping within a cruciform plan with central and side aisles.

7   A small group with side aisles and light and access at the ends. Seats curved for better visual lines.

8   A raised platform about a rectangular space serving as seating area, with access at the center of the sides. Lighted from above or artificially.

9   A large group on an inclined or curved floor within a rectangle, with central and side aisles. End ingress with side exits. Seats curved for better visual lines. Artificial light.

10 Two combined groups on an incline within a rectangle with artificial light. Curved seats and an entrance at one end.

11 A group divided by parallel aisles and inclined floor. Entrance to auditorium and rostrum. Overhead or artificial lighting.

12 Curved seats within a hexagonal enclosure, with radiant and parallel aisles. Overhead or artificial lighting.

13 Seats on an inclined or stepped floor, with a central aisle divided by an inclined approach to the rostrum. Lighting at the rostrum end.

14 Seats curving about a semi-circular rostrum, with side aisles. Access from side aisles and rostrum.

15 Curved seats within a rectangle divided by parallel aisles. An entrance at the end serving the seats and an inclined passage serving the rostrum.

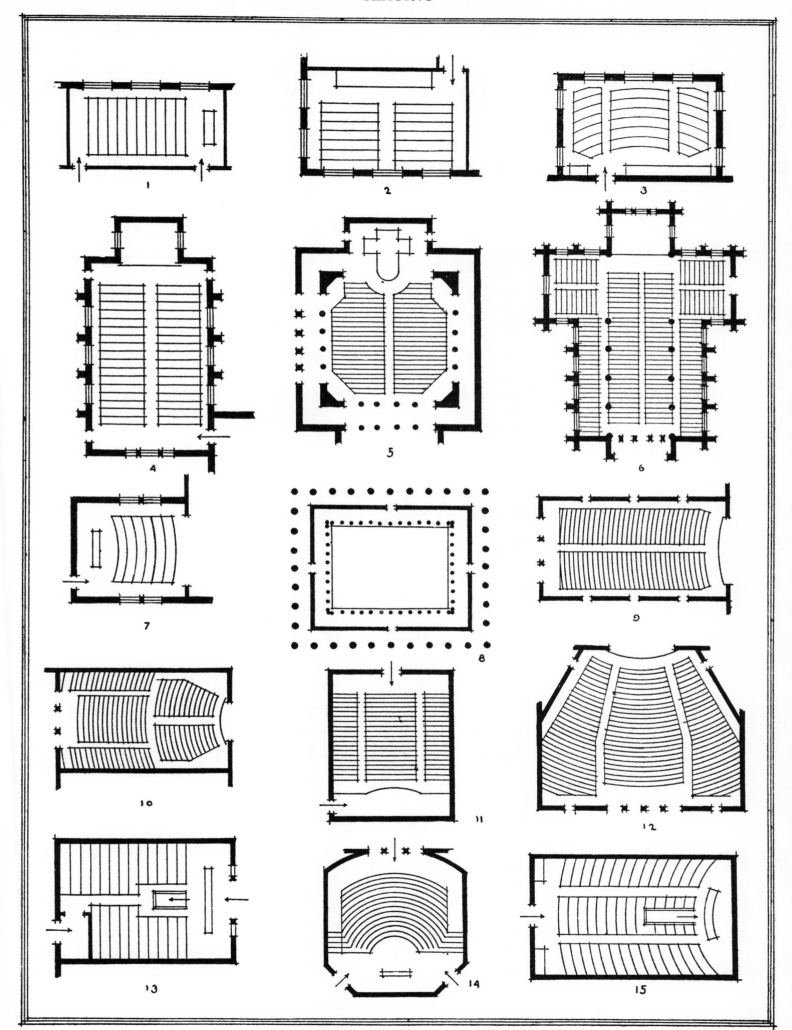

Plate 51

SEATING

Dealing with inclined and stepped floors, enclosed, semi-enclosed and open structures

1   A central and side aisles within a rectangular space, entrance at the end of the auditorium and side of the rostrum.   Light at side.

2   The same in principle as 1 but with the seats curved.

3   A group within a rectangle with converging aisles dividing the group, with light from the sides and access from the rostrum.

4   A group within an octagon with a stepped central aisle leading to the apex of a triangular rostum.   Seats parallel to the adjacent sides of the platform with minor parallel aisles perpendicular to the platform sides.

5   Stepped seats arranged in a semi circle in an open area with radiant aisles in front of a raised platform or stage.

6   Stepped seats with a semi-circular end plan at the end of an open arena.

7   Stepped seats arranged on the sides of an open rectangular arena.

8   Stepped seats within an elliptical space with radiant aisles before a stage.

9   A. Stepped seats around an elliptical arena with access from the highest tier and openings at varying lower levels.

    B. Stepped seats about an ellipse with access from radiant aisles and inclined passages at varying levels.

    C. Stepped seats about an ellipse with radiating aisles and a monumental passage.

    D. Stepped tiers about an elliptical arena, the tiers used as seats without aisles.

10   Stepped seats and aisles about an oblong arena with a circular end.

11   A combination of curved and stepped seats within a semicircular enclosure.

12   Level and banked seats within a semi-circular enclosure in combination.

13   Level and banked seats within a semi-circular enclosure in combination with two minor flanking enclosures.

14   Seats upon an incline within a rectangle in combination with banked seats at the sides.

15   Level and banked seats before a platform within a semi-circular auditorium with minor semi-circular spaces on the circumference.

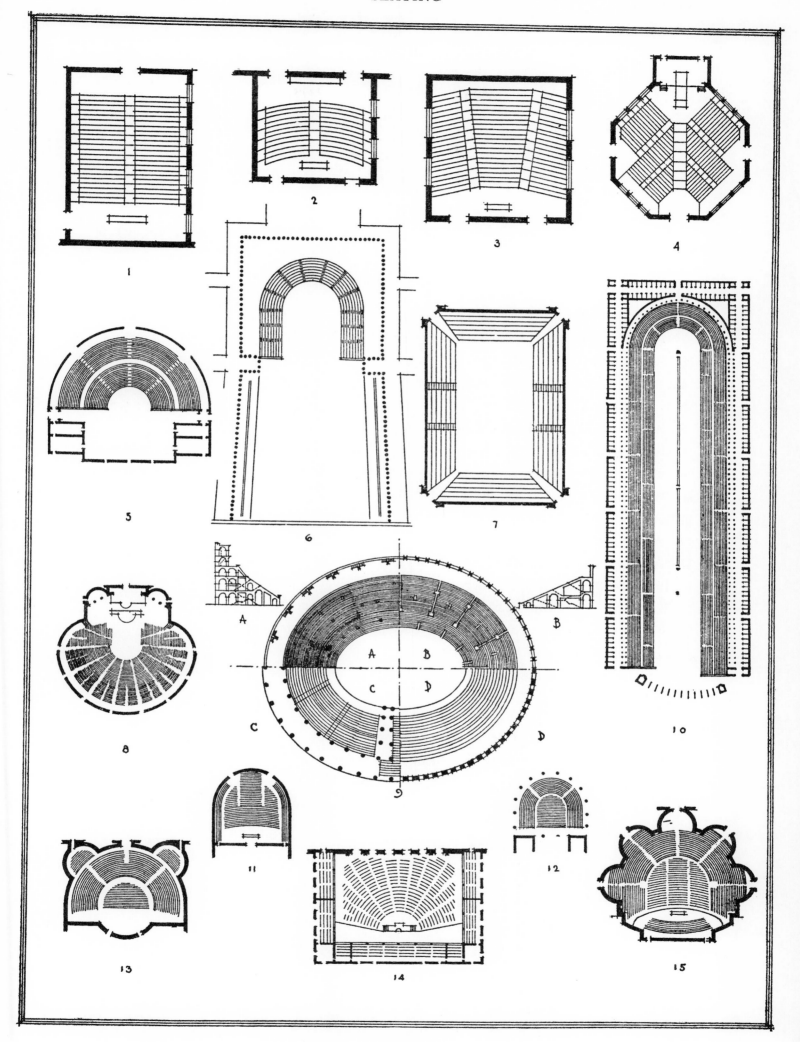

Plate 52

STAIRS

The stair is a series of steps, or flights of steps, for passing from one level to another, or several successive levels, with or without connecting landings between levels.

Dealing with interior stairs

1   A run with a return between flights.

2   A stair radiating from a newel.

3   A spiral mast stair with self-supporting risers.

4–5–16   Circular stairs with well and outer string as the supporting member.

6–17   Elliptical stairs with open well.

7   Stairs within an octagonal space.

8   Stairs with a semi-circular end return.

9–14–15   Stairs within a rectangle and two corner landings.

10   Stairs within a square with corner landings.

11   A run with radiating start and termination.

12   A straight run.

13   A semi-elliptical run with a central landing.

18–19–20–24–35   Divided flights with central preliminary runs.

21–22–23   Balanced runs at the sides of a rectangular space.

25   Balanced runs within a rectangular space having semi-circular ends.

26   Balanced runs within a circular space.

27–28   Central preliminary runs with balanced secondary runs within semi-circular end spaces.

29   Balanced circular stairs at two corners of a rectangle.

30   Straight parallel runs starting at the opposite ends of a rectangular space.

31   Symmetrical circular stairs at the sides of a vestibule.

32   A spiral stair with landings.

33   Semi-circular stairs at the ends of a rectangular space, with diagonally opposite starting points.

34   Three parallel runs with alternating starting points.

36   A double helical stair.

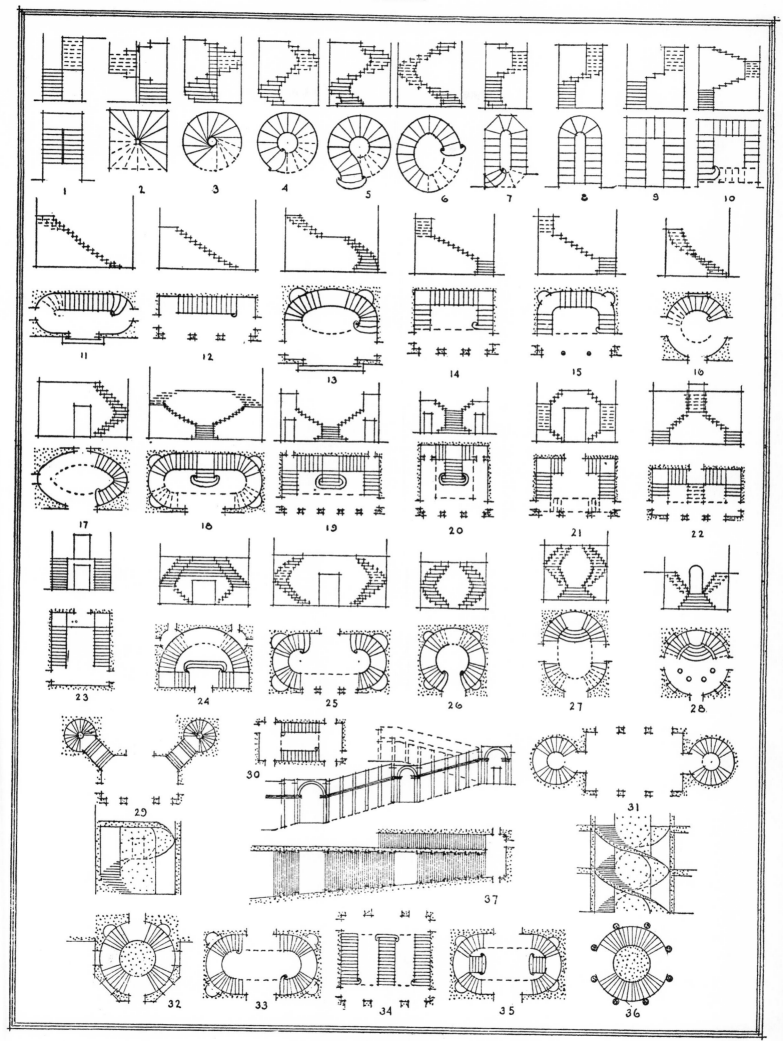

Plate 53

STAIRS

Dealing with the exterior stairway

1   A central landing with divergent runs to circular corner landings.

2   Steps at the center and ends of a walled enclosure.

3   Semi-circular central steps in composition with a balustrade.

4   Steps and landings with semi-circular ends beyond and behind a terrace wall.

5   Steps and landings beyond a wall continuing between the wall.

6   A wall with an entrant curve with projecting semi-circular steps continuing between the wall.

7   A run with circular ends continued between projecting walls.

8–10   Steps at the corners of a balustraded terrace.

10   Steps leading to a central platform from which two semi-circular runs start, being connected at their centers with lateral runs.

11   A right angled run in a jog in a wall landing on a stepped platform.

12   Steps and landing projecting beyond and within the corner of a wall.

13–14   Stepped platforms at the corners of a wall with divergent runs.

15   Diverging landings at the ends of a wall with runs parallel to the wall.

16   A corner landing with runs at right angles with each other.

17   Masked runs at a wall opening.

18   A projecting monumental platform with semi-circular runs at the sides.

19   An entrance in a wall with lateral runs.

20   A lateral run with triangular treads.

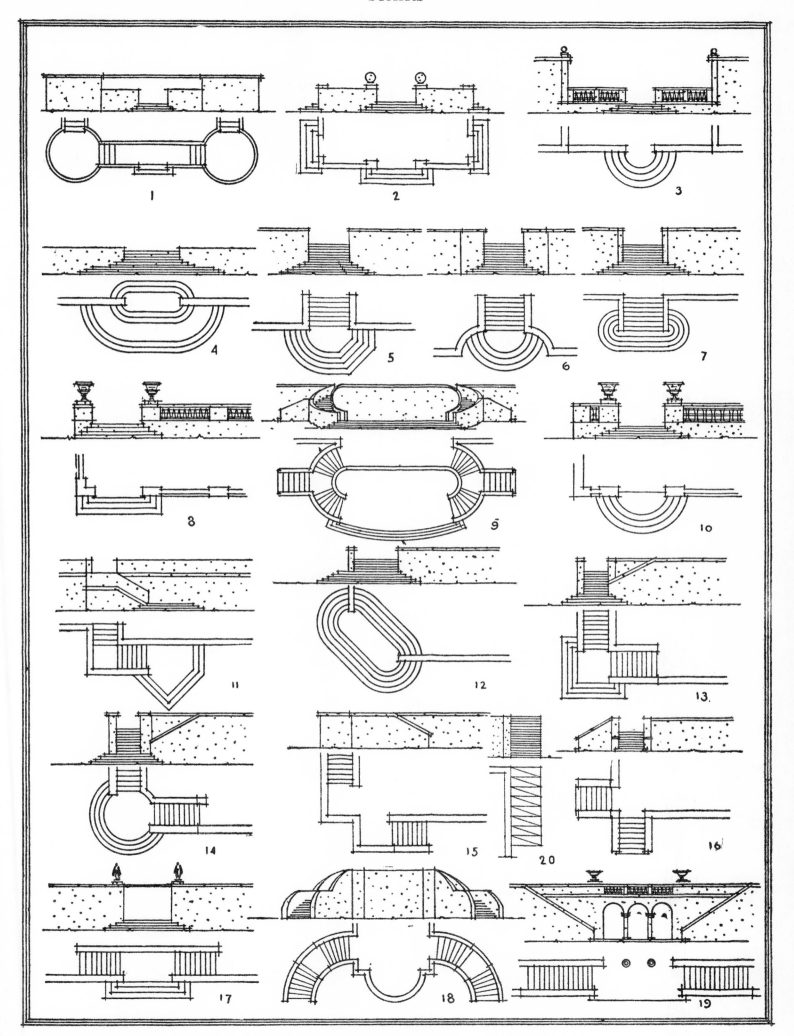

Plate 54

STAIRS

Dealing with the exterior stairway

1   A common starting point with side runs returning about the landing.

2   Runs starting at the ends and meeting at a central landing and returning to separate landings.

3   Rectangular runs meeting at a central landing.

4   Double corner runs meeting at a central landing and continuing.

5   A projecting wall with steppings used as a stair.

6   Projecting semi-circular runs with a central landing.

7   A straight run upon a segmental arch.

8   A broken run upon a segmental arch.

9   Straight runs and winders in combination.

10 Corner landings with runs at right angles, one flight meeting at a common monumental landing from which a central run starts, while the other continues in a straight line to the final level.

11 An exterior spiral staircase about a solid core.

12 Grouped semi-circular and "S" runs about a semi-circular landing.

13 Central and side runs with common secondary landings leading to a third and fourth landing.

14 Entrant-angle runs with a common upper landing.

15 An arcaded run perpendicular to a wall.

16 An arcaded double run meeting on a common upper landing.

17 A right angled run at the corner of a building and a wall.

18 Runs from a common point to separate landings.

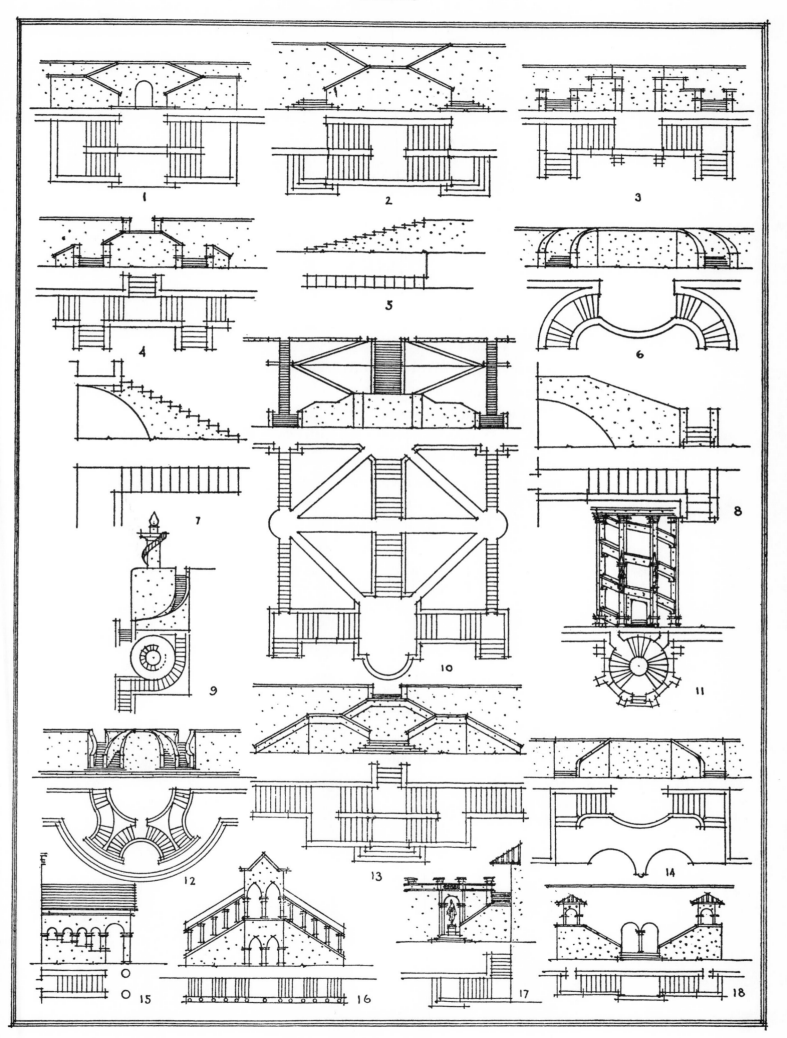

Plate 55

STAIRS

Dealing with the ramp

1 Lateral ramps meeting a semi-circular stair.

2 A single central straight ramp flanked by parallel side ramps leading to a higher level.

3 Ramps and stair beginning at a common spot.

4 Straight and right angled ramps in combination.

5 Circular stair at ends of a terrace in combination with corner diagonal ramps.

6 Semi-circular lateral ramps, with separate approach.

7 "S" shaped lateral ramps with common approach.

8 Ramps with a common starting point with lateral runs and returns.

9 Ramps with semi-circular turns serving two levels.

10 Quarter and semi-circular turns in combination with a stair.

11 Quarter circle ramps with a central landing, with dissymmetrical returning ramps with landings above the central landing.

12 An inclined approach with sharp quarter turns at the entrant angles of the walls of the building.

13 A single zig-zag ramp in combination with a straight stair with a common starting point.

14 A double intersecting zig-zag ramp in combination with a central stair and parallel end ones.

15 A ramp ascending the walls of a stepped edifice.

16 A spiral ramp about a solid core.

17 Ramps along the inner side walls of a square tower.

18 Intersecting double ramps with stair and step compositions.

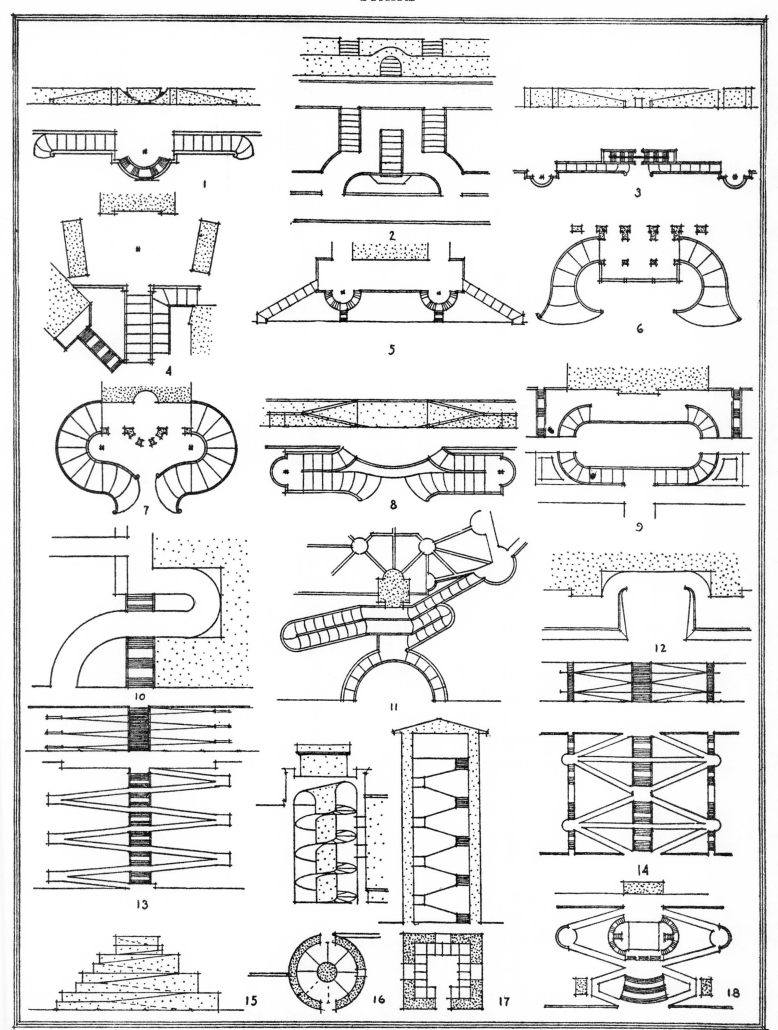

Plate 56

TOWERS

The tower is a structure, isolated or incorporated, of any form or plan in which the vertical dimension greatly exceeds the lateral.

Dealing with turrets and various tower terminations

1   A square wall turret, supported upon a shaft.

2   A round corner turret supported upon a shaft.

3   A round corner turret supported upon corbeling.

4   An octagonal tower in an entrant angle.

5   Superimposed circular towers with an octagonal tower at the side.

6   A round tower with a smaller one at the side.

7   A round tower in an entrant angle with a corner turret.

8   A composition with a round tower, small side tower and side wall.

9   A tower motive at the corner of a projecting wall.

Terminations

10   A spire with corner turrets.

11   A composition with wall turrets and a cupola.

12   A superimposed tower with corner turrets connected with flying buttresses.

13   Superimposed towers with a balcony feature.

14   An octagonal arcade and spire termination.

15   A parapet around a spired canopy motive.

16   A double termination, an octagonal arcade above a low hipped roof.

17   A superimposed octagonal tower with an octagonal cupola above a square.

18   A superimposed tower and cupola, with corner console buttresses.

19   A square tower with a corbeled parapet as a termination.

20   A loggia motive with a flat hipped roof.

21   A round tower with superimposed parapets and conical roofs.

22   An octagonal arcade with a spire and cupola.

23   A pediment with ridge roof.

24   Coupled arches with a saddle back roof.

25   Gables with a ridge roof.

26–33   A square spire with two slopes to the hips.

27   A square spire with gables on two sides.

28   A square tower with a spire having concave hips.

29   A roof with concave hips with a cupola and bulbous dome.

30   A hipped spire with three rakes.

31   A domed termination with cupola.

32   A combination of gable, dome and spire.

34   A pyramidal roof with a horizontal band.

35   A hipped roof with an octagonal cupola and concave corner chamferings.

36   An octagonal spire with an upper terminal feature.

37   Bulbous domical terminations.

38   A hipped spire with dormers, corner chamfers and end emphasis at the ridge.

Plate 57

TOWERS

Dealing with those having vertical diminance

1   A round tower with superimposed smaller towers continuing at the side.

2   A square tower with a corbeled parapet.

3   A square tower with an octagonal continuation.

4   A square tower with a round side tower and an octagonal continuation.

5   A square tower with a half gable and a pent house roof.

6   A square tower with batter walls, upper bays and a ridge roof.

7   A square tower with an arcade and low hip roof.

8   A square tower with two gables and a ridge roof.

9   A square corner tower with a gable feature at the top.

10   A tower with semi-circular ends and a hip roof with a ridge.

11   A square tower with a decagonal arcade and dormered spire.

12   A square tower with upper balconies and a two-storied hexagonal continuation.

13   A square tower with a superimposed round tower and conical spire.

14   A tower with diagonal salients, conical continuation and cupola.

15   A tower with buttresses at the corners and a hipped spire.

16   A tower with vertical members, superimposed arcades, corner turrets and spire.

17   A tower with vertical members, an arcaded attic and a spire.

18   A tower with buttresses at the corners and a chamfered spire.

19   A tower with buttresses at the corners and center, with corner turrets, flying buttresses, and a spired octagonal central continuation.

20   Superimposed octagonal towers continuing from a chamfered square.

21   A tower with vertical members and a loggia terminal motive with a drum and spire.

22   A tower with receding canopied vertical members, with superimposed smaller towers and a crested spire.

23   A square tower with vertical members and a pedimented superimposed arch motive with a bulbous roof termination.

24   A tower with a batter wall base and corner and central salient features with canopies and a high hip roof with a ridge.

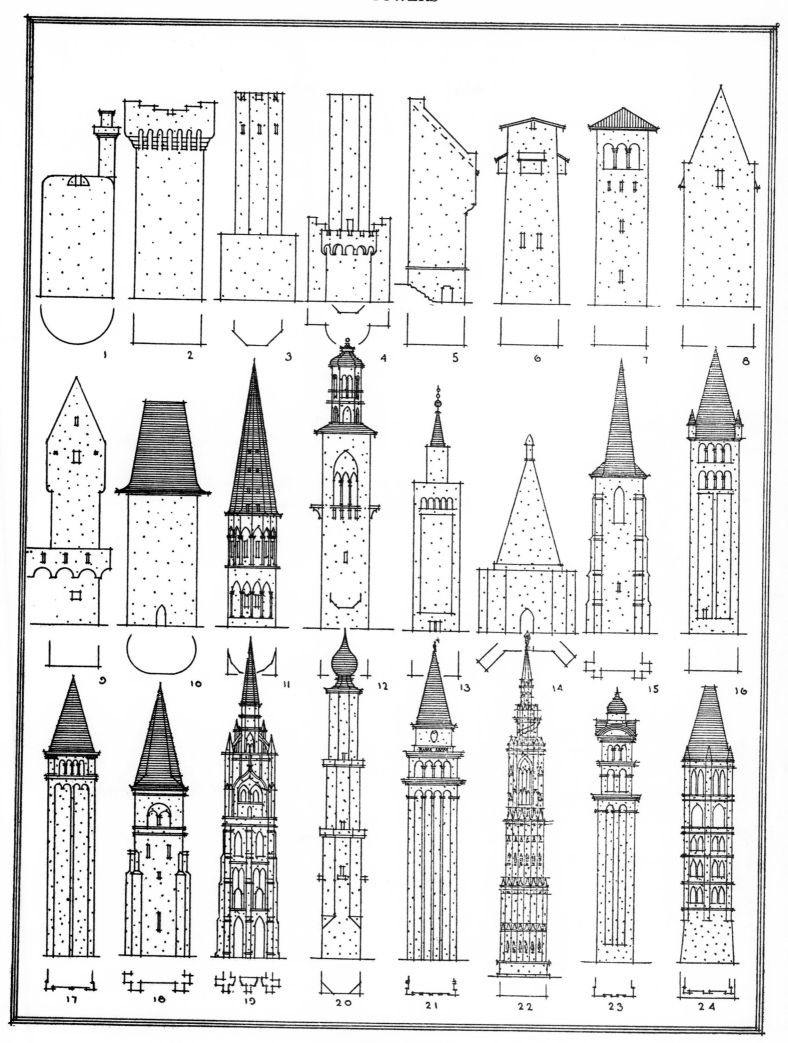

Plate 58

T O W E R S

Dealing with those having a horizontal expression

1 Superimposed diminishing towers.

2 Round tower with batter wall base, horizontal bands and conical roof.

3 Coupled round towers with horizontal bands and conical roofs.

4 Coupled round towers with horizontal bands and a terminal octagonal with concave sides and parapet.

5 Superimposed diminishing towers with bases and cornices.

6 A tower with an arch and superimposed coupled arches, horizontal bands and a low hipped roof.

7 A cruciform tower with stepped sides and roofing, gables and cupola.

8 A tower with corner turrets and horizontal bands.

9 A tower with a lower arch and upper arcade, horizontal bands and a low hip roof.

10 A sloping round tower with pedestal, base and cap motive with small side towers and a central cylindrical feature.

11 A tower with receding buttresses at the corners, horizontal bands and parapet.

12–16 A tower with receding superimposed roofs with concave ridges.

13 A round tower with sloping walls and horizontal divisions.

14 A tower with end buttresses, superimposed arcades, horizontal courses, cornice and pyramidal roof.

15 A tower with superimposed courses and cornice, with corner and central features.

17–21 Superimposed arches and horizontal courses, cornice and low hip roof.

18 Superimposed round towers with parapets.

19 Superimposed receding masses with cornices with an octagonal termination.

20 Superimposed arches with horizontal cornices, corner turrets and a central domed roof.

22 Receding corner buttresses, superimposed cornices and low chamfered spire.

23 A tower with superimposed colonnades and low hip roof.

24 A tower with horizontal bands and low hip roof.

25 A tower with horizontal divisions, cornice and parapet and central feature.

26 Superimposed arcades, horizontal bands and cornice with a central conical termination.

27 A tower of superimposed receding colonnades.

28 A tower with horizontal bands and cornice with an arcaded attic and arcaded octagonal termination.

29 A round tower with an arcade at the base and top with a connecting spiral arcade treatment.

30 An octagonal tower with a small round side tower, with horizontal bands and cornice on the larger tower and spiral bands and arcade motive on the smaller tower.

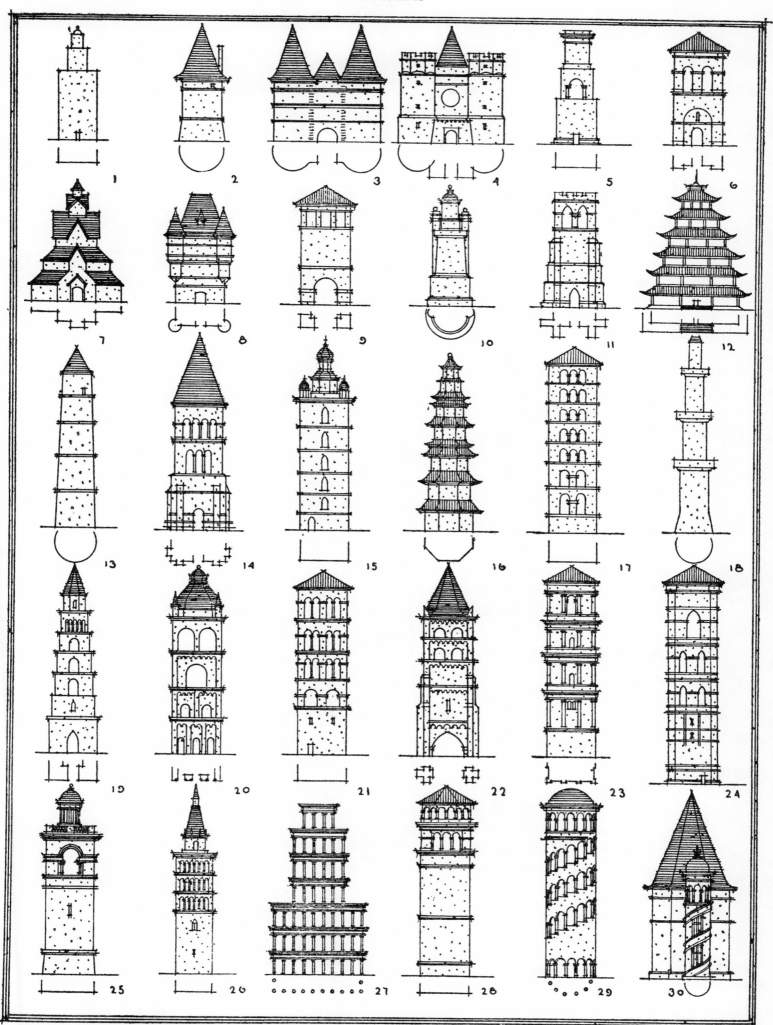

Plate 59

VAULTS

The vault was primarily a series of arches in combination used as a covering, as a ceiling or a roof. It may also be used to carry a roof, a floor or stairs.

Dealing with the simple vaults

1 The circular Barrel, Tunnel, Wagon or Cradle vault.

2 The Elliptical Barrel vault.

3 The Segmental Barrel vault.

4 The Pointed vault.

5 The Rampant vault.

6 A barrel vault with Skew arch. Semi-circular or semi-elliptical cross section, spiral joints with warped surfaces.

7 A Conoidal or Expanding vault. Used mostly in transitions from the square to the octagon.

8 A Convex-Conoidal vault. Used mostly in compound vaults.

9 An elevation of an expanding vault.

10 A barrel vault flanked by semi-barrel vaults.

11 A Domical or Spherical vault.

12 An Annular or Truncated Spherical vault.

13 Showing the mechanical principle of the Byzantine or Spherical pendentive.

14 A domical vault upon pedentives in combination with end convex-conoidal vaults and semi-domical vaults.

15–19 A domical vault supported upon arches whose heads are higher than the spring of the dome.

16–17 Examples of Domes with uninterrupted pendentives supported by arches.

18 A dome upon a drum supported by pendentives springing from splay faces.

20 A dome supported by pendentives springing from splay faces.

21 An intersection of a smaller with a larger barrel vault.

22 An intersection of a small barrel vault with a domical vault.

23 Intersecting barrel vaults of unequal diameters springing from the same level, called Welsh or under pitch vaults. The groin line of intersection is an hyperbola.

24 A pointed arch intersecting a barrel vault.

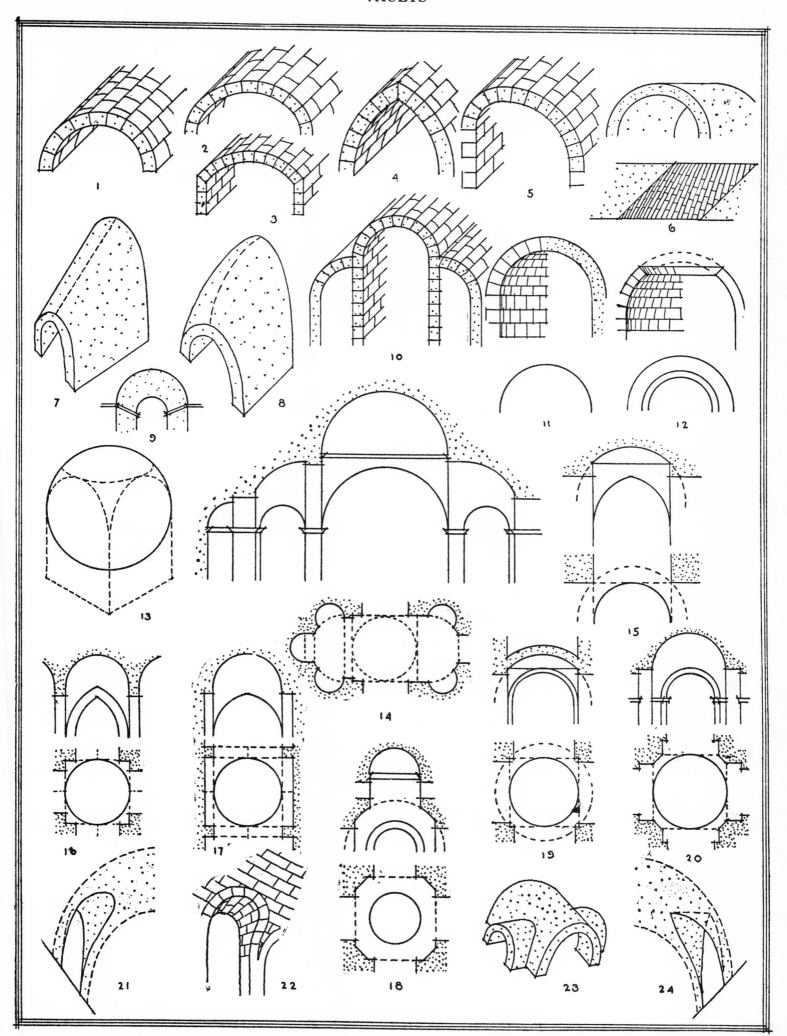

Plate 60

VAULTS

Dealing with the compound vault

Vaults formed by the intersection at right angles of two or more equal ones of any cross section, are known as Groined vaults. The salient angle formed by the intersection being the groin. When the arch is composed of four parts of equal barrel vaults with reentrant internal angles, the arch is called Cloistered.

1-2-21-23 Quadripartite vaults formed by the intersection of two barrels, pointed or expanding vaults, for covering a square surface.

3-5-15-20 Underpitch or Welsh vault. Arches springing from same level, but with incomplete intersection. For covering oblong surfaces.

5 A Stilted vault. Of unequal components, the smaller stilted so that the ridges will have the same level.

6-7-13-14-16-17 Tracery vaulting. 6-13-14 Conoidal in form, 7-16-17 Pyramidoidal.

8 Segmental vault, with equal or unequal components.

9 A Segmental main vault intersected by a semi-circular transverse vault.

10 Groined and Cloistered vaults in combination with an octagonal opening at the ridge.

11 A Rampant vault. The intersecting of two barrel vaults, one of them inclined.

12 Tripartite vaults. Formed by the intersection of three barrel or expanding vaults. Singly and in combination with quadripartite vaulting, the latter covering polygonal surfaces.

18 Vault with lateral and groin ribs only.

19 Groined vault with unequal components covering an oblong surface.

22 Half a quadripartite vault springing from corner columns. Half a quadripartite vault with a circular penetration.

24 An octagonal surface vaulted with a central shaft.

25-26-27-28-29-30 Various vaulting compositions used in apsidal vaulting.

Plate 61

VAULTS

Dealing with the ribbed vault

The Ribbed Vault—Vaults constructed with the rib as the chief structural member supporting the panels in between. This method of vaulting may be divided into two classifications, Simple and Compound. The former with the diagonal wall, transverse ribs, while to the latter is added intermediate, cross and interrupted and intersecting liernes.

1–2–3   Showing the principle of rib construction and methods of supporting the panels.

4   Diagonal ribs and convex ridges between arches of unequal height.

5   Plan of Diagonal or Groin ribs.

6   Diagonal ribs with arches of same height, examples of horizontal and sloping ridges.

7–8   The spring of various ribs, a Diagonal, b Wall, c Transverse.

9–10   The construction of a Pendant Rib vault.

11–12–13–14   Vaults in which the Diagonal ribs are omitted.

15–16–18   Quinquipartite vaults, 15–18 covering a pentagonal space and 16 covering a trapezoid.

17   A vault with ridge ribs.

19   A Hexapartite vault.

20   A Quadripartite vault with oblique side vaults.

21   Panel vaulting.

22   A Septempartite vault.

23–24–25   Octopartite vaulting.

26   Groin ribs not meeting at the center, but terminating at the corners of an octagon.

27–28   Star vaulting.

29   An example of Diagonal and Cross ribbing.

30–31   Examples of fully developed ribbed vaults.

33–34–35–36–37   Various compositions with intermediate ribs.

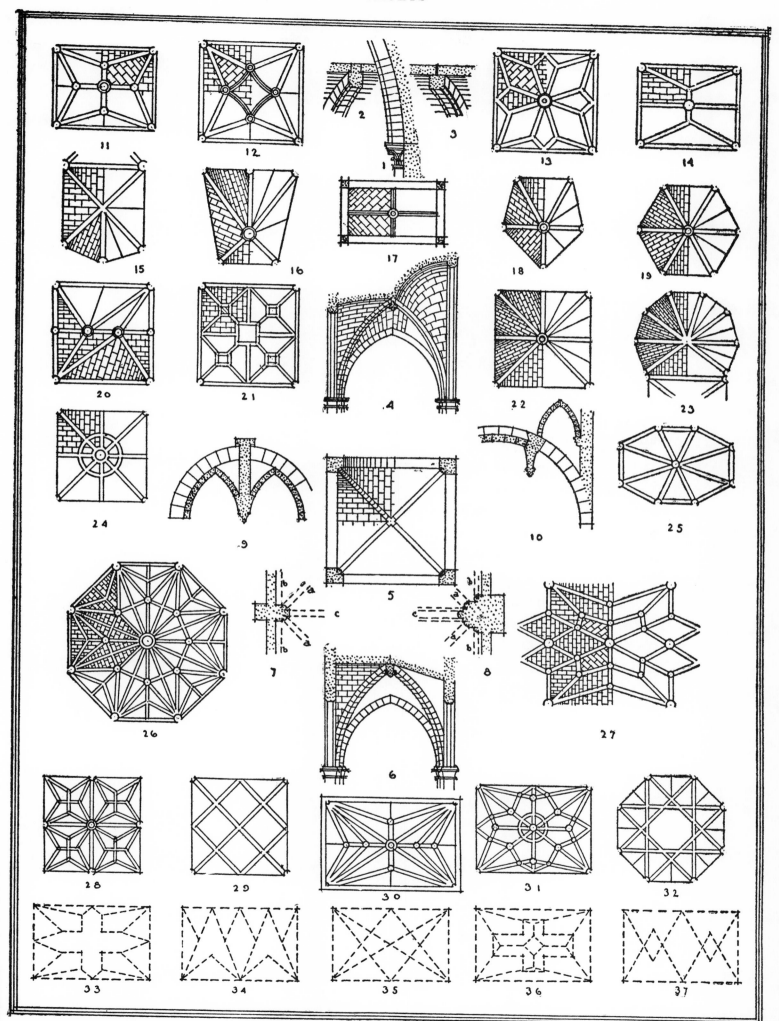

Plate 62

VESTIBULES

The vestibule is an intermediate chamber or passage between the entrance and interior or court of a building, serving as a shelter or place of accommodation.

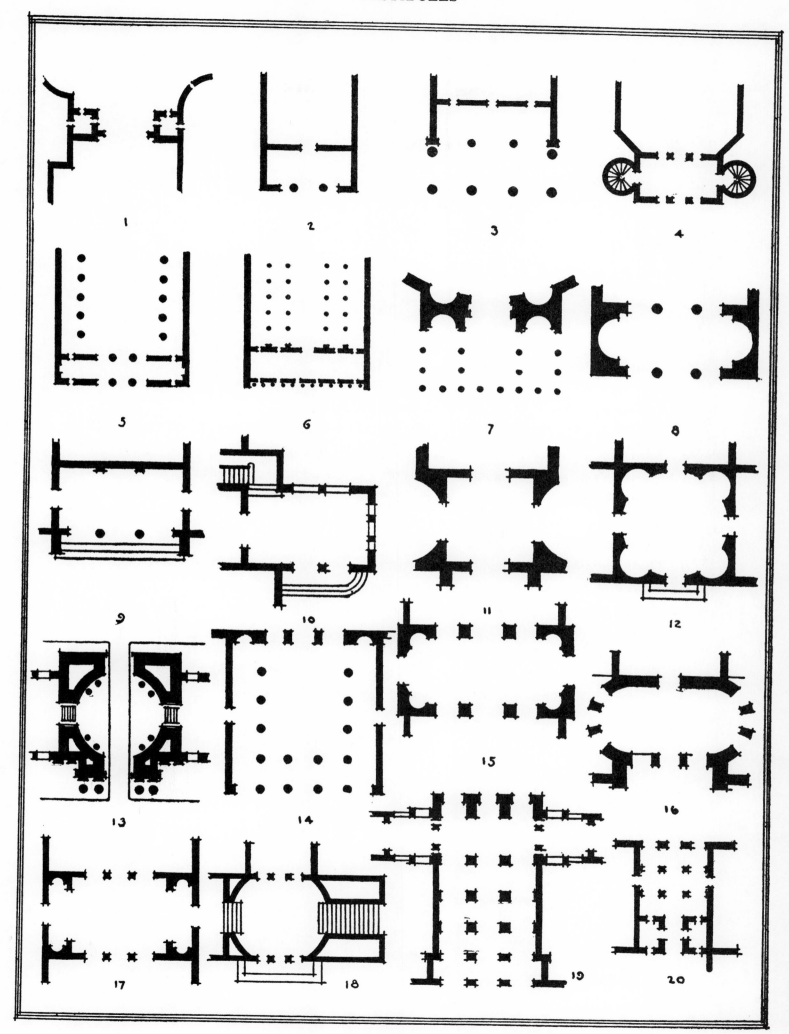

Plate 63

VESTIBULES

1   A passage serving as vestibule for two separate buildings.

2   Three openings arranged symmetrically with the lateral ones of greater importance.

3   A balanced arrangement of openings with dissymmetrical stairs.

4   A vestibule as an independent composition with lateral ones of lesser importance.

5   An exterior arcade used as a vestibule.

6   A series of vestibules of varying importance in combination.

7–8   Balanced motives for flanking stairs, in a building or serving two buildings.

9   The main vestibule serving as a passage and serving secondary lateral openings.

10   A vestibule with surrounding corridors, with dominant lateral emphasis.

11   An important architectural feature screening a balanced vestibule motive, which is itself placed off axis.

12   A vestibule with eight balanced openings.

13   A vestibule as a large chamber serving a concealed stair and a corridor.

14   A colonnaded vestibule between cloistered means of communication.

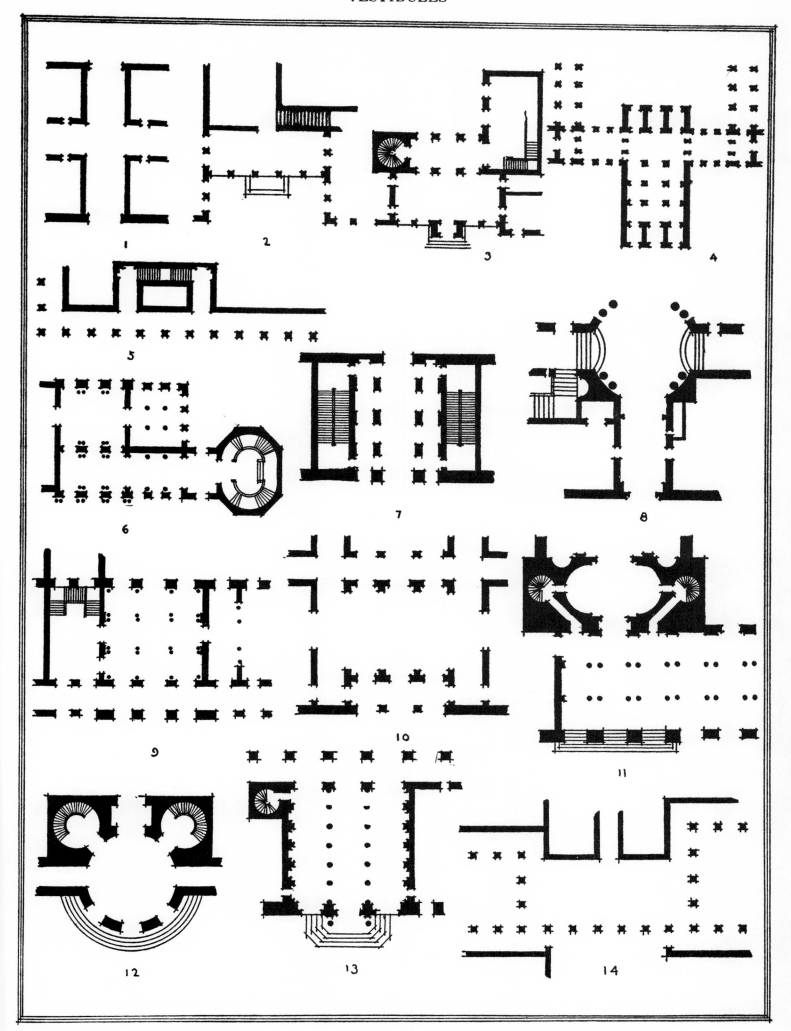

Plate 64

WALL TREATMENT

The wall is the side of a structure serving to enclose a room, house, or other space and serving to carry the floors and roof in many cases. It may be built of masonry, iron, or wood and its treatment varies according to the material employed and its own peculiar limitations.

Dealing with the treatment of the surface

1–4   Alternating textures of the same material.

2   Rustication, with various designs.

3   Bands with alternating textures or material.

5   Horizontal bands.

6   A diaper of alternating stone, tile, or tile and stone, or colored marble.

7   A diaper of brick and tile, marble, stone or terra-cotta.

8   A surface of decorated tile.

9   A diaper of brickwork. Contrasting color, surface or projection.

10   A design in brick of contrasts in color, or projection.

11   Bevelled rustication.

12   Rustication and terra-cotta or marble disks.

13   Surface treated with designs in high relief.

14   Masonry with a pattern of carved projecting objects.

15   Panelled and bevelled rustication.

16   Brick bands with concrete and pebbles.

17–18   Fresco, painted or mosaic, surface enrichment.

19   Mouldings framing painted ornamentation.

20   Horizontal projecting bands of masonry.

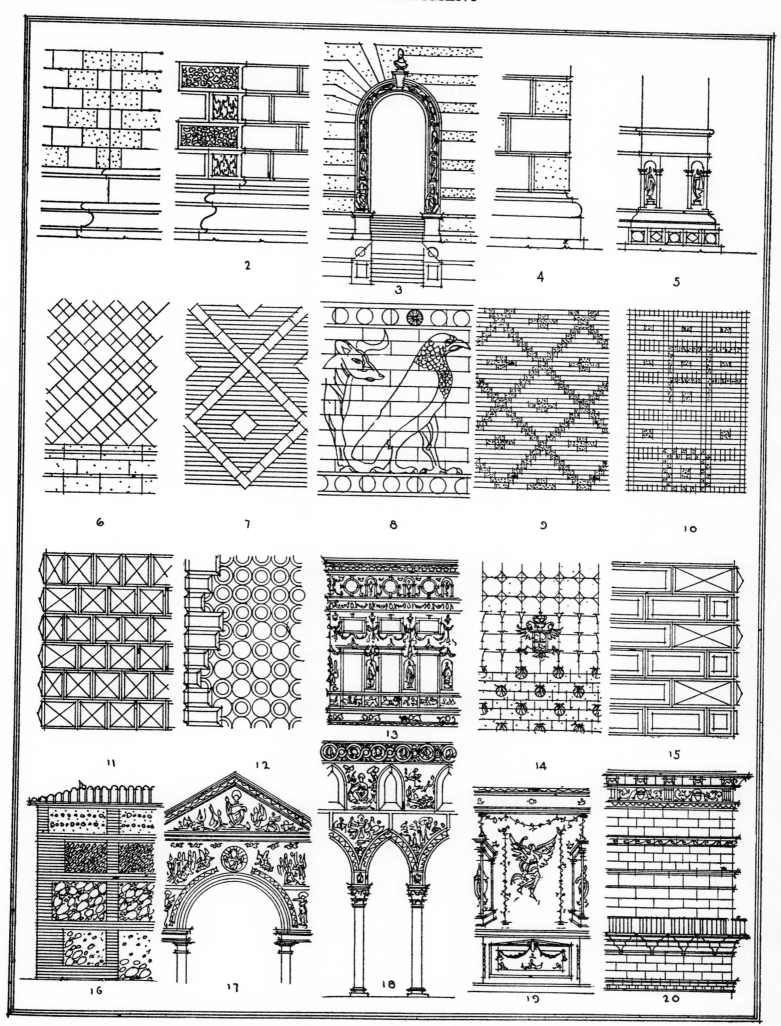

Plate 65

WALL TREATMENT

Dealing with surface embellishment

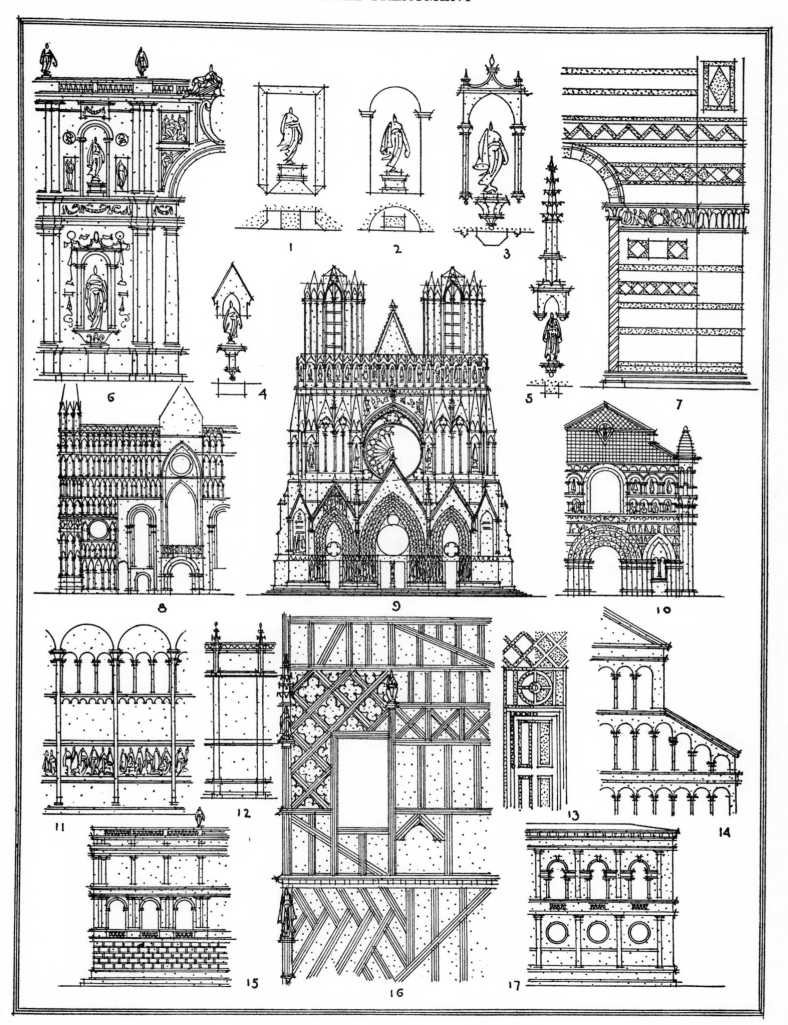

Plate 66

WALL TREATMENT

Dealing with the termination of the wall

1 A plain coping of masonry or terra-cotta.

2 A ridged coping of slate or tile.

3–4–5–6–7–8–9–10–11 Various examples of crenelated battlements.

12 A battlement above a corbeled string course.

13–14 Examples of crenelations.

15–16–20–21 Structural members projecting beyond the wall to support a cornice or the roof rafters.

17 The wall terminated as a parapet with openings for embellishment.

18 A parapet of pedestals and statuary.

19 Vertical members projecting and forming a crested coping.

22 A series of corbeled arches supporting horizontal bands in a cornice composition.

23–24 Examples of arches springing from corbels and supporting the roof.

25 Architrave, frieze and cornice as a termination.

26 The horizontal broken by a pediment and projection for special emphasis.

27–28–29–30 Pedimented compositions for terminations on attics or dormers.

31–32 Pedimented dormer motives.

33 A gable treated with superimposed orders and semi-circular pediments.

34 A pediment terminating a gable.

35 A broken pediment as a gable with the central part further emphasized with a similar motive.

36 A pediment crowning a gable flanked with consoles.

Plate 67

WALL TREATMENT

Dealing with the treatment of the corner

1–2–3–4   Examples of quoins or corner rustication.

5   A vertical rusticated motive, in combination with horizontal features.

6   Coupled orders, with a vertical continuation of rustication.

7   A rusticated colonnade with a vertical continuation of rustication.

8   Superimposed coupled orders with a parapet and statuary.

9   A single order with attic and statuary.

10   A turret or tourelle emphasizing the corner.

11–16   Types of corner buttresses.

12   An attenuated order.

13–14   Corner niches with canopies and statuary for special emphasis.

15   Twisted columns in an entrant angle, with spring courses placed above one another.

17   Twisted columns with an elaborated termination of storied canopies and spire.

18   An octagonal, square, or round tower used for corner strength.

19   A square tower with wall niches and a canopy and spire termination.

20   Canopied niches grouped at the corner of a building.

21   A niche in a reentrant wall angle.

22   Ornament in high relief placed on the corner angle. Arms, brackets, sconces, statuary, etc.

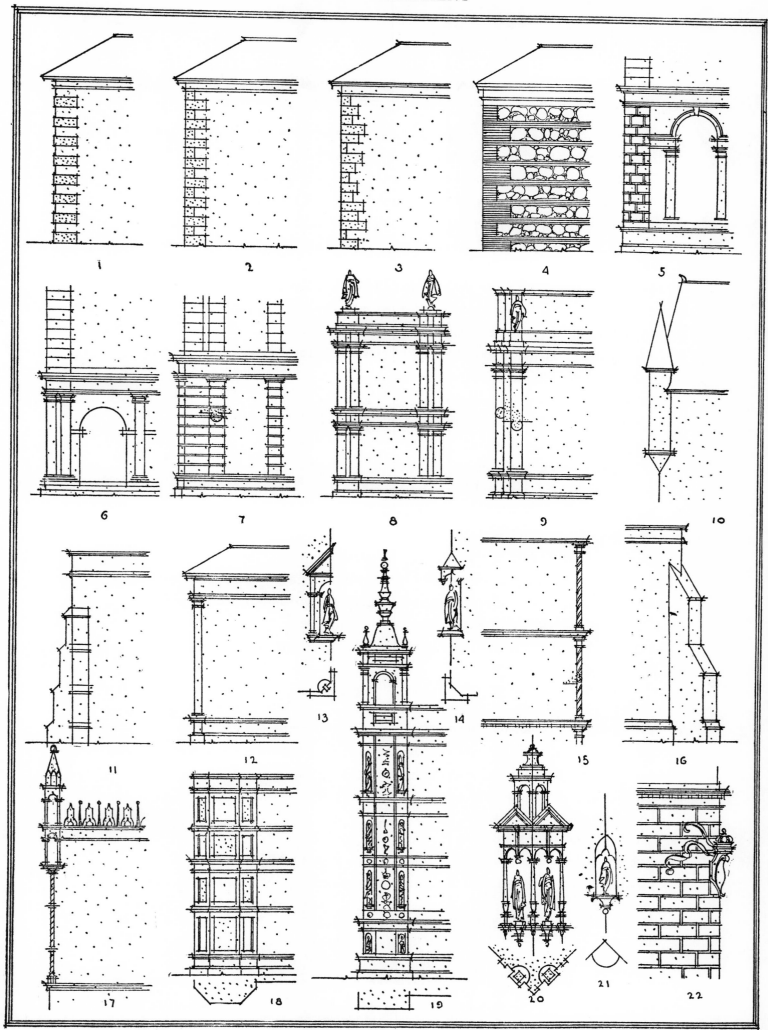

Plate 68

WINDOWS

The window is an opening for the admission of light and air into the interior of a building. Broadly used, the term includes the openings and their architectural treatment.

1–3–4–11–21–25–26–27   Various examples of windows enclosed with an architrave.

2–32   Openings with projecting mouldings at the head and sides.

5–6–10   Openings with sloping sides, plinths, architraves and cornices.

7   An opening framed with an architrave having a frieze and pediment.

8–9   Examples having sills, architraves, side consoles and an entablature or pediment.

12   An arched opening with side columns, upon a projecting pedestal motive crowned with an entablature.

13–14–15–16   Openings flanked with columns having pediments, and with sill motives.

17   An opening with a pendent head, flanked with columns supporting a semi-circular cornice.

18   A pointed opening with flanking columns and splay sides at the head.

19   Superimposed openings with flanking columns and crowning members.

20–23–24   Openings in salient panel compositions.

22   An opening in a broken pediment composition.

28–30–31–33   Cusped openings with splay sides.

29   A splayed cruciform window.

32   A pointed opening with splayed reveal and head moulding.

34   An opening with compound head and splayed reveal.

35   An opening with ornamental cusped openings.

36   Coupled pointed windows.

37   Coupled round headed openings with a dividing column.

38–41   Arches enclosing coupled openings having flanking and central columns.

39   An opening in a stepped pediment motive divided by transom bar and mullion.

40   Coupled openings in a three column portico composition.

42   Pointed coupled windows with cusped heads and piercings, within a pointed arch having side and central columns.

43   An opening with central and side mullions forming an overhead composition with cusped openings.

44   Triple arched openings upon columns, with greater height at the center.

45   Examples of "Rose Windows." Radiating arched and circular mullion compositions.

46–51   Openings divided in three parts by mullions. Muntin casement divisions.

47   Three openings with greater height at the center connected by mullions and a transom bar.

48   Three pointed arches enclosing square headed openings.

49   Round headed arches with separating columns within a trefoil arch.

50   Pointed arches upon columns with cusped overhead piercings within a square or oblong opening.

52   An arched opening divided into two pointed openings, with four subdivisions in each arch produced by alternating mullions and columns. Cusped piercings forming an overhead tracery motive.

53   An opening with a mullion and superimposed transom bars, and muntined casements.

54   A rectangular opening with mullion and transom bar divisions with muntined casements.

Plate 69

WINDOWS

Dealing with the bay window

1 A salient feature of frame and glass with an overhead protecting motive.

2 A rectangular salient with windows and hip roof.

3 A five-sided salient upon diagonal wall supports.

4 A salient rectangular motive upon brackets.

5 A bay window supported upon brackets with a central salient feature.

6 A grilled opening with a bay window feature.

7 A bay window upon brackets in a gable.

8–16 A bay window upon a corbel feature.

9 A bay window upon a center bracket in a jerkin headed roof gable.

10 A bay window upon brackets, with a curved roof and cupola.

11 A double salient bay window upon a corbel.

12–13 Three-storied examples supported upon corbels.

14 A corner example upon wall supports.

15 A corner turret example supported upon a shaft.

17 A bay window supported upon a corbel with a domical termination and architecture around the window opening.

18 A two-storied triangular bay window supported upon a shaft.

19 A rectangular salient with pedestal and entablature and emphasized sash divisions.

20 A semi-circular example with conical roof.

21 A semi-circular example with a hip roof.

22 A three sided bay window with a hip roof.

23 A rectangular salient bay window with a base hip roof, mullion and superimposed transom bars.

24 A three sided bay window with a gable head.

25 A gabled bay window above an entrance, supported upon columns.

26 A two-storied bay window with horizontal features.

27 Bay windows of unequal height in combination, flanking an entrance.

28 A three-sided two-storied bay window with a gable termination.

29 A three-sided bay window with vertical window tracery.

30 A five-sided three-storied bay window with a projecting roof gable as a termination.

Plate 70

Dover Books on Art

THE FOUR BOOKS OF ARCHITECTURE, Andrea Palladio. A compendium of the art of Andrea Palladio, one of the most celebrated architects of the Renaissance, including 250 magnificently-engraved plates showing edifices either of Palladio's design or reconstructed (in these drawings) by him from classical ruins and contemporary accounts. 257 plates. xxiv + 119pp. 9½ x 12¾. 21308-0 Paperbound $10.00

150 MASTERPIECES OF DRAWING, A. Toney. Selected by a gifted artist and teacher, these are some of the finest drawings produced by Western artists from the early 15th to the end of the 18th centuries. Excellent reproductions of drawings by Rembrandt, Bruegel, Raphael, Watteau, and other familiar masters, as well as works by lesser known but brilliant artists. 150 plates. xviii + 150pp. 5⅜ x 11¼. 21032-4 Paperbound $6.00

MORE DRAWINGS BY HEINRICH KLEY. Another collection of the graphic, vivid sketches of Heinrich Kley, one of the most diabolically talented cartoonists of our century. The sketches take in every aspect of human life: nothing is too sacred for him to ridicule, no one too eminent for him to satirize. 158 drawings you will not easily forget. iv + 104pp. 7⅜ x 10¾. 20041-8 Paperbound $3.75

STYLES IN PAINTING, Paul Zucker. By comparing paintings of similar subject matter, the author shows the characteristics of various painting styles. You are shown at a glance the differences between reclining nudes by Giorgione, Velasquez, Goya, Modigliani; how a Byzantine portrait is unlike a portrait by Van Eyck, da Vinci, Dürer, or Marc Chagall; how the painting of landscapes has changed gradually from ancient Pompeii to Lyonel Feininger in our own century. 241 beautiful, sharp photographs illustrate the text. xiv + 338 pp. 5⅝ x 8¼. 20760-9 Paperbound $6.50

PAINTING IN ISLAM, Sir Thomas W. Arnold. This scholarly study puts Islamic painting in its social and religious context and examines its relation to Islamic civilization in general. 65 full-page plates illustrate the text and give outstanding examples of Islamic art. 4 appendices. Index of mss. referred to. General Index. xxiv + 159pp. 6⅝ x 9¼. 21310-2 Paperbound $7.00

THE MATERIALS AND TECHNIQUES OF MEDIEVAL PAINTING, D. V. Thompson. An invaluable study of carriers and grounds, binding media, pigments, metals used in painting, al fresco and al secco techniques, burnishing, etc. used by the medieval masters. Preface by Bernard Berenson. 239pp. 5⅜ x 8. 20327-1 Paperbound $4.50

THE HISTORY AND TECHNIQUE OF LETTERING, A. Nesbitt. A thorough history of lettering from the ancient Egyptians to the present, and a 65-page course in lettering for artists. Every major development in lettering history is illustrated by a complete aphabet. Fully analyzes such masters as Caslon, Koch, Garamont, Jenson, and many more. 89 alphabets, 165 other specimens. 317pp. 7½ x 10½. 20427-8 Paperbound $5.50